Religions for Peace

A Call for Solidarity
to the Religions of the World

FRANCIS CARDINAL ARINZE

DOUBLEDAY

New York   London   Sidney   Auckland

PUBLISHED BY DOUBLEDAY
a division of Random House, Inc.
1540 Broadway, New York, New York 10036

DOUBLEDAY and the portrayal of an anchor with a
dolphin are trademarks of Doubleday,
a division of Random House, Inc.

Book design by Ralph Fowler

Library of Congress Cataloging-in-Publication Data
Arinze, Francis A.
Religions for peace : a call for solidarity to the
religions of the world / Francis Arinze.
p.   cm.
Includes bibliographical references.
ISBN 0-385-50460-8
1. Peace—Religious aspects.   I. Title
BL65.P4A75   2002
191'.7873—dc21
2001053879

FIRST EDITION
1 3 5 7 9 10 8 6 4 2

Contents

Preface

The following reflections on *Religions for Peace* were written in the beginning of the year 2001. As they are about to go to print, a catastrophic and heartrending attack was unleashed on New York and Washington, D.C., on September 11, 2001.

We are all sad. We pray. We mourn the thousands dead. We offer sympathy to many more wounded, bereaved, made unemployed, ruined in their business, or disoriented in life. We also seek answers.

This painful moment makes the reflections proposed in this little book all the more urgent. All may not agree on the motivation of the perpetrators of the disaster. Is it a feeling of injustice, oppression, repression, exclusion, or even racist behavior? Or are the reasons political, economic, or cultural? Are there unhealed historical memories?

Whatever may be the motivation, one thing is clear. Healthy religious considerations are needed to face this present tragedy in a way that respects the natural ordering of God the Creator and does honor to humanity. We must also do our best, people of all religions together, to prevent such a disaster ever happening again.

There are some religious considerations that could serve as a guide for our reflection and action. God is the creator of all humanity. In following his will, inserted into human nature guided by right reason, is the peace for all men and women.

Human life is sacred. It must be protected. We have no right to kill ourselves or to kill innocent people. While self-defense is a right and is justifiable, it has to be kept within due limits.

Justice, peace, and tranquillity in the world are built on the pillars of respect for the fundamental rights of other people, especially their right to life, religious freedom, and free exercise of political, economic, and cultural rights. Economic and political development of peoples is also an obligatory road to peace. If people are illiterate, under-developed, oppressed and repressed, then justice and peace are rendered more difficult.

Violence, terrorism, the taking of human lives, and the destruction of property are condemned by all genuine religions. They are acts opposed to love of God and neighbor. No matter the problems and challenges to be faced, these violent roads are the wrong ones. Solutions in line with respect for God and humanity have to be sought, no matter how difficult and long-term they may be.

All religions are bound to help their followers to engage in reflections such as these. May this book, *Religions for Peace*, be of some service in this important task.

Francis Cardinal Arinze
SEPTEMBER 28, 2001

Foreword

Few themes merit greater attention and action on the part of both the governments of the world and religious authorities as the one treated in this timely sheaf of essays entitled *Religions for Peace*, now offered to a wider readership. For this collection, Francis Cardinal Arinze draws from his vast and deep experience of dialogue with men and women of various religions and beliefs and diverse cultures. This book contains precious insights demonstrating in clear and concise terms how a genuine rapport with God cannot but engender love and harmony in one's relationship with one's fellow human beings and, in fact, with the whole of creation. This golden truth is enshrined not merely on cold dead tablets of stone but in the heart of every human being.

The book systematically studies the relationship between religion and peace. Cardinal Arinze digs into what I term *common ground* and the unprejudiced reader of any religious persuasion will readily endorse the ideas expressed in these pages. Anchored firmly in Catholic tradition and teaching, these reflections are set forth in a manner that is crisp, clear, concrete, and courageous. The chapters are closely linked flowing one into the next, thus making reflections both cohesive and compact.

But peace is not just a job to be done. Neither can it be achieved, as Cardinal Arinze rightly admits, by human effort or religions alone. It is primarily a gift from above, to receive which, one must pray and be rightly disposed. More than a finished product, peace is a process always in the making. And because the peacemaking never ends, peace remains a constant challenge. It is here that cultures play a crucial and contributory role. After all, no religion exists in a void but is always rooted in culture and is its transcendent element. The dialogue between religion and culture and among cultures themselves can assist this process and, by dismantling the structures of prejudices, promote peace, understanding, and love. The edifice of peace, at once so precious and precarious, can only be grounded on the firm foundation of an ethic of solidarity, of a sense of belonging, of mutual love and respect, and the upholding of fundamental human rights.

Fanatics and fundamentalists have no doubt given religion a bad name. Politicians, having their own hidden agendas, at times exploit religion to fan the flames of intolerance and hatred. Such unwholesome propaganda can only boomerang, causing a spiraling effect of violence. Cardinal Arinze advocates a change of heart and attitudes, and real repentance, and invites goodwill on the part of all who, while accepting their own religious identity and diversity as well as responsibility for past mistakes, must in all humility and honesty seek reconciliation and join hands to build bridges of friendship and fellowship over troubled waters.

The thoughts contained in *Religions for Peace* are not just academic and abstruse conjectures of an idle bystander. They are practical, pastoral, and personal, coming as they do from one, who, for more than a decade and a half as President of the Pontifical Council for Interreligious Dialogue at the Holy See, has been actively engaged in this field. Cardinal Arinze speaks from wisdom born of experience and proposes the thesis that the dialogue between religions, like that between cultures, not only can but must contribute toward a culture and civilization of peace. Who can deny the inevitable and inseparable link between religion and culture? While religion is at the very heart of culture, the latter is the womb into which religion is conceived and lives. There exists between these two realities a healthy symbiosis, when they are combined and harnessed, they make up a formidable force for peace.

However, while governments can strain to negotiate peace and draw up peace proposals and religions strive to promote peace, it is the individual human being who, in the last analysis, is the bearer of peace. It is not merely a truism to say that peace begins with you and me. Each of us is either a peacemaker or a peace-breaker. We know very well that interpersonal conflicts stop only when intrapersonal conflicts cease for disturbed persons. He who is at peace with himself in turn learns to live in peace with others. He who desires peace must learn to love, and he who loves generates peace. What is said of individual persons can, mutatis mutandis, be applied to society and nations at large.

Coming as it does in the wake of the new Christian millennium, so rich with promise, it is my hope and prayer that this book will challenge the reader of any religious affiliation and culture with the conviction that peace is not just a utopia but is possible, and that the religions of the world, despite—and I like to add—*because* of the diversity of their tenets and traditions, cultures and customs, have an invaluable and indispensable contribution to make toward the peace process. I deem it indeed a personal and particular privilege to pen these lines to introduce *Religions for Peace* and wish to affirm that adherents to any religion or faith who are honestly engaged in the quest for peace will find in these pages much enlightenment and encouragement.

Paul Cardinal Poupard
PRESIDENT, PONTIFICAL
COUNCIL FOR CULTURE

Introduction

Peace strikes a responsive chord in the hearts of the followers of the religions of the world. Christians have the custom of exchanging a sign of peace. Muslims interpret the name of their religion, Islam, as referring to peace, *salām*. Jews greet each other by saying *shalom*, "peace." Buddhists want to promote peace. So do Sikhs. So do the followers of the Traditional Religions. In my seventeen years of engagement in the promotion of interreligious dialogue, I have not come into contact with the follower of any religion who does not regard his or her religion as in favor of peace.

And yet there is tension. There is violence. Even war has now become an all too common part of our daily lives. What have religions to say about this harsh reality? And in any case, what peace exactly are we talking about? What is peace? The religions of the world all extol peace. Why then do some people accuse these religions of being the cause of tension and even war? Moreover, since religion is such an important dimension of culture, do we think that interreligious and intercultural relations are likely to lead to clashes rather than to harmony?

It is also useful to ask ourselves what the various religions can actually do to promote peace, both by way of inculcating attitudes and by taking practical initiatives. What role should the religions give to prayer for peace?

To show that the foregoing considerations are not mere theory, it is helpful to list some existing interreligious initiatives for peace on the international level. As I am a Catholic, I shall also mention some of the things that the Catholic Church has done and is doing for peace promotion, while suggesting that the reader of a differing religious family may also spell out the contribution to peace of his or her religious community.

In all these reflections it will become clear that a fundamental requirement for peace is respect for the human right to religious freedom and that this right deserves express treatment.

We shall conclude by stating that this book does not want to say that the religions alone can build peace. Other promoters of peace are also needed. As humankind steps into the Third Millennium, it aspires for peace and on its knees begs God for this perfect gift.

ONE

Understanding Peace

THE ESSENCE OF PEACE

When we say "peace" we mean the tranquillity of order. We mean that situation of justice and rightly ordered social relationships that is marked by respect for the rights of others, that provides favorable conditions for integral human growth, and that allows citizens to live out their lives to the full in calm and joyful development.

The peace we are talking about, therefore, has such components as freedom, truth, and stability. It includes the integral development of the human person, of the whole person, and of all persons. It implies interdependence between people, an interdependence that is not just tolerated but is freely accepted and generously lived. In short, true peace rests upon mutual love and benevolence between people and supposes a serene society in which these people live.

Peace, therefore, is a very positive concept. It is not mere passiveness. Rather is it an active commitment to establishing an order that will be a source of tranquillity. This attitude is greatly helped by a recognition that all human beings belong to one family, that they have one Creator and a single origin, that human nature is the same in all people, that they have all been redeemed by Jesus Christ, and that they are all called to the same final destiny.

Within this human family, the will of God the Creator is that each person should respect the rights of others and be willing to work with them as fellow pilgrims on the journey of life. But this respect for the rights of others flows from the spirit of justice, and therefore justice is absolutely necessary for true and lasting peace. This justice can manifest itself, for example, in respect for life from the moment of conception right up to natural death, in respect for the weak and the defenseless, in respect for the right to religious freedom for individuals and for groups, and in the elimination of discrimination against people because of their language, social status, ethnic origin, color, or sex. It also shows itself through respect for the equality of citizens, especially as exercised by civil administrators.

Peace is therefore not a negative concept. It is no mere absence of war. It is much more than that. If a country spends heavily on its army and on instruments of war, piles up sophisticated weapons including nuclear arms, and then turns around and tells us that it is doing all this in order to preserve peace in the world, we are really being presented with another understanding of peace. What that country really means is that it is piling up weapons of destruction in order to discourage or even defeat or damage severely any other country perceived as a competitor, a threat, or a danger. This is the same as saying that by a buildup of terror, its aim is to frighten any other country away from the idea of attacking it. If that other country behaves in a similar way, we have a perfect case of a balance of terror. This is not peace.

The ancient Romans had a proverb: "If you want peace, prepare for war." That may look wise in the face of an apparently incurable human propensity to resort to arms as one of the most primitive ways to try to settle a conflict. But to accept this thesis as inevitable would be to regard human society as a terrible jungle full of wild animals in which the stronger attack and eat the weaker. But a more careful consideration of the moral, religious, and cultural heights to which human beings can rise, advises us that a more optimistic view of human nature is viable.

There is another state of tension, sometimes called "the war of nerves." It does not consist necessarily in the imminent explosion of armaments, but in a constant fear of this that eventually wrecks the nerves of the parties concerned. Obviously the existence of such a war of nerves is not a situation of peace. Even the mere absence of such a state of fear would not be enough to qualify for peace.

Peace is something really positive. It has to include a certain tranquillity of mind and heart that guarantees security. It is the peace of which the prophet Isaiah speaks: "Integrity will bring peace, justice give lasting security. My people will live in a peaceful home, in safe houses, in quiet dwellings" (Is 32:17–18). Jesus Christ promises this peace to his followers as a divine gift: "Peace I bequeath to you, my own peace I give you, a peace the world cannot give, this is my gift to you" (Jn 14:27).

THE DESIRE OF THE HUMAN HEART

Peace is the desire of the human heart. The unfettered human aspiration is toward respect for one's rights and those of others and the recognition that other human beings are unique individuals who should never be reduced to means or considered as mere instruments, but who should be respected and accepted as persons, as subjects of rights and duties.

All peoples, languages, cultures, religions, and social groups understand peace and have a special word for it.

They appreciate the meaning of wholeness, health, safety, security, well-being, justice, order, calm, and the fulfillment of desire. They do not want disturbance, disorder, insecurity, instability in society, abnormal conditions, tension, violence, or war. Moreover, they do not want to labor under oppression, injustice, or violation of rights, nor to suffer from underdevelopment.

The human spirit, or the human heart in popular language, is most important in our consideration of where peace, or the lack of it, originates. War does not lie primarily in armaments or missiles. It arises from the human heart. The human conscience, convictions, systems of thought to which one is bound, and also the passions which influence one, form the seedbed of war or peace. It is in the conscience or heart that one is sensitive to the absolute values of goodness, justice, rectitude, brotherhood, and peace. It is also in the depths of the heart that a person can reject or ignore the appeals of these absolutes.

THE VALUE OF PEACE

Peace is a necessary requirement if people are to grow and reach the height of their potential. Peace is not an optional climate for human life and growth—it is a necessity. It is, as Pope John Paul II has said, "the primary objective of every society and of national and international life" (*Message for World Day of Peace*, 2001, n. 18). "Nothing is lost by peace. Everything can be lost by war," as Pope Pius XII wisely observed in his August 24, 1939, radio message just before the outbreak of the Second World War (in *Discorsi e Radiomessaggi di S.S. Pio XII,* vol. 1, p. 306).

The world today cannot be unconcerned by the alarming increase in arms and their power to wreak destruction. The commitment to nuclear nonproliferation is sometimes halting. Not only governments but also paramilitary groups, terrorist organizations, and even individuals seem at times to be overcome by the temptation to violence.

Many developing countries are wasting their scarce resources in armaments and huge armies that they call defense. Their true development is thereby slowed down if not indefinitely postponed. National and social cohesion and harmony are threatened by interethnic tensions and civil wars. There are stories and rumors of rebellions planned or actually carried out. Families are scattered and their members separated. Both city dwellers and village farmers are forced to become refugees. Some children have not seen one year of peace or quiet schooling. Faced with such threats, who does not appreciate the value of peace and the need to promote it?

PEACE A RARE COMMODITY

No matter how much the human heart desires peace, it would seem that peace is a rare commodity in the market of human history, especially in our times. The twentieth century has been called "history's bloodiest century." Sadly, there are grounds that seem to justify this. The century has known two terrifying world wars. It is the century of the Holocaust, of so-called ethnic cleansing, and of cruel tribal massacres. Humankind has known bruises, hurts, wounds, pains, and avoidable collisions. It is calculated that since the end of the Second World War, humanity has not known up to a hundred days of effective peace. Most of the time, in some part of the world, there has been a war going on, whether a clash between nations, or a civil war, or continuous guerrilla warfare. Or there are racial conflicts, violent clashes, acts of terrorism, assassinations, massacres, or murders in some part of the globe. Hardly does a day pass without human blood being shed by someone in the world. The first pages of the Bible, the Jewish and Christian Holy Book, tell us about Cain, who, out of envy, killed his brother Abel (cf. Gn 4:3–8). It is unfortunate that many people follow in the footsteps of Cain.

According to one reckoning, in 1993 there were sixty wars going on in the world, with some of them having some religious coloring. Most of these wars were to be found south of the equator, with Africa claiming twenty-five of them, Asia twenty-four, and Latin America five (cf. *L'Actualité Religieuse dans le Monde*, 110, April 15, 1993, p. 32). One can readily understand how much these wars not only provoke violence and destruction but also retard the development of whole peoples and regions. Between 1950 and 1990, it is estimated that fifteen million people died in war or as a result of war (cf. *Aggiornamenti Sociali*, 2 [1999], p. 135).

It is not without reason that the twentieth century has been called a century of wars, with intervals not so much of peace as of truce.

As humanity steps into the third Christian millennium, it cannot ignore the dark clouds that overshadow its bright hopes, nor the open wounds that are not yet healed. Not only are there many bitter conflicts raging in parts of the earth, but societies are finding it increasingly difficult to maintain solidarity and harmony among people of different religious, racial, linguistic, and cultural backgrounds who for various reasons now live and work together. While this plurality is more pronounced in the big cities, it is not absent elsewhere. In many parts of Europe and North America, for instance, the influx of refugees from conflict areas such as Somalia, Bosnia, Sudan, Rwanda, Afghanistan, and Kosovo in the past decade has stretched the resources of the host societies and could cause tension if care is not taken.

PEACE A PERPETUAL CONQUEST

Seeing, therefore, how rare true peace can be in human society, it follows that effort to build peace has to be sustained, while resisting discouragement and fatigue. In spite of the lofty aspirations of peoples and religions, peace in the concrete is not easy to realize. For human beings wounded by original sin inherited from Adam and by personal sins, and consequently prone to selfishness and forgetfulness of the rights of others, and not always up to carrying out clearly recognized duties, peace remains a perpetual conquest to be achieved. And for Christians, it is a gift to be obtained from God on our knees in prayer.

As Pope Paul VI put it: "Peace cannot be limited to a mere absence of war, the result of an ever precarious balance of forces. No, peace is something that is built up day after day, in the pursuit of an order intended by God, which implies a more perfect form of justice among men" (*Populorum Progressio*, 76).

The promotion of peace has therefore to be on the top of the agenda of humanity in every age, and more so in our times when communication among peoples has reached a level never attained before. Not only religious leaders and statesmen, but also academicians, professionals, and indeed every human being ought to be concerned about peace promotion. Since religion is a major dimension of human life, let us now explore what the various religions have to say on the subject of peace.

Religions Extol Peace

The religions of the world are agreed on this, that all extol peace. I have not met people of any religion who say that they not in favor of peace.

RELIGION:

VERTICAL AND HORIZONTAL DIMENSIONS

To be sure, the primary idea in religion is not the promotion of peace but the worship of God. Religion refers in the first place to the relationship of the creature to the Creator. By religion we acknowledge that God made us, that we want to live according to his will and that we seek contact with him. Therefore, most religions include a body of beliefs, a code of conduct, and a ritual of prayer.

But this vertical dimension of relationship with God also calls for the horizontal dimension, which refers to how we relate with our fellow human beings. Christianity summarizes this second aspect of religion by saying that the person who loves God must also love the neighbor (cf. 1 Jn 4:20). A good Christian is a good citizen. The building up of the kingdom of heaven not only does not abstract from, but positively promotes and demands the building up of the earthly city or the kingdom of this world (cf. Vatican II: *Gaudium et Spes*, 42, 43).

If religion did not come to grips with the realities of the human condition on earth, if religion did not try to meet the challenges of alienation and reconciliation, of hurt and healing, of war and peace, then religion would be declaring itself marginal in life. Religion would be relegating itself to the background in society. Religion would be presenting itself as perhaps an interesting philosophy, but one that is wholly detached and unconcerned with the sometimes beautiful, sometimes harsh realities of human existence on earth.

The truth is different. Religions all through human history have seen it as their duty to deal with concrete human situations and experience. They are convinced that their belief in God, the Creator, the Transcendent, the Way, or the Supreme Spirit, does engage them to make a contribution toward the healing of the world, and therefore toward the building of peace.

With admirable unanimity, the religions of the world teach the Golden Rule: Love your neighbor as yourself. This is a key foundation for peace.

The love of one's neighbor, which Christianity professes as the golden rule of moral conduct (cf. Mt 7:12: "Always treat others as you would like them to treat you; that is the meaning of the Law and the Prophets"), is also part of the doctrinal patrimony of other great world religions. I quote here the maxims of six of them:

> *Hinduism*: This is the sum of duty: Do not do to others what would cause you pain if done to you.
>
> —MAHABHARATA 5.15.17

> *Buddhism*: Hurt not others in ways that you would find hurtful.
>
> —UDANAVARGA 5:18

> *Confucianism*: It is the maxim of loving kindness (Jin): "Do not unto others what you would not have them do unto you."
>
> —ANACLECTS (RONGO) 15:23

> *Judaism*: What is hateful to you, do not do to your fellow man. That is the entire Law; all the rest is commentary.
>
> —TALMUD, SHABBAT 312

Islam: "No one of you is a believer until he loves for his brother that which he loves for himself."

—THE FORTY-TWO TRADITIONS OF AN-NAWAWI

African traditional religion: What you give (or do) to others, these will give (or do) to you in return.

—RWANDAN PROVERB

If the followers of the world religions sincerely lived the Golden Rule, one of the major foundations for peace would be laid.

RELIGIONS SPEAK EXPLICITLY ABOUT PEACE

The religions that humanity has known speak explicitly about peace. They extol it. They inculcate it. They stress its importance.

Since one-third of humanity today is Christian, let us first examine what Christianity says about peace. Thereafter, we shall see what the other major religions say on this topic.

CHRISTIANITY ON PEACE

Peace is given a key place in the religion established by Jesus Christ. Already in the Sermon on the Mount, the "manifesto" of the Kingdom of God that Jesus was inaugurating, Jesus praises the promoters of peace: "Happy the peacemakers: they shall be called sons of God" (Mt 5:9). When he sent his disciples to spread his Good News, Jesus instructed them to call down peace on people: "Let your first words be, 'Peace to this house!' And if a man of peace lives there, your peace will go and rest on him; if not, it will come back to you" (Lk 10:5–6).

The peace that Jesus promised would, in the final analysis, be a gift from God: "Peace I bequeath to you, my own peace I give you, a peace the world cannot give, this is my gift to you" (Jn 14:27). St. Paul was later to write about the peace of God, which surpasses all understanding (cf. Phl 4:7), and of the "fruits of the Spirit," of "what the Spirit brings," which include peace, patience, kindness, and forbearance (cf. Gal 5:22).

Jesus himself often gave his disciples the peace greeting "Peace be with you" (cf. Jn 14:27; 16:33; 20:19,21,26; Lk 10:5) and exhorted them not to be afraid (cf. Mt 8:26; 28:5; Jn 6:20).

After all, the Prophet Isaiah had earlier in prophecy described the coming Savior as "Prince of Peace" (cf. Is 9:6) and the Psalmist had said that in Christ justice and peace would abound (cf. Ps 72:7).

The Apostles, especially St. Peter and St. Paul, followed the teaching of Jesus. They greeted the people with peace (cf. Phil 4:7; II Thes 3:16; I Pet 1:2; 5:4; II Pet 1:2; III Jn 15; Jud 1:2; Apoc 1:4).

St. Paul wrote the Romans that they were to love everyone, including their enemies. They were to avoid seeking revenge. "If your enemy is hungry, you should give him food; and if he is thirsty, let him drink. Thus you heap red-hot coals on his head. Resist evil and conquer it with good" (Rom 12:20–21). Paul in this was following on the clear teaching of Jesus: "You have learned how it was said: Eye for eye and tooth for tooth. But I say this to you: offer the wicked man no resistance. On the contrary, if anyone hits you on the right cheek, offer him the other as well; if a man takes you to law and would have your tunic, let him have your cloak as well. And if anyone orders you to go one mile, go two miles with him. Give to anyone who asks, and if anyone wants to borrow, do not turn away" (Mt 5:38–42). This doctrine is not weakness. It is strength. Can we just imagine what profound peace the world would know if everyone welcomed and lived this doctrine?

The peace, therefore, that Christianity extols demands love of God and neighbor and requires a constant combat against egoism. It also includes willingness to carry one's cross and follow Christ. Indeed, St. Paul calls Christ "our peace" (Eph 2:14) because by his suffering and obedience, Christ defeated the power of Satan and of death, overcame man's separation from God, and reconciled Jews and Gentiles to one another and all to God.

In the history of the Church, St. Augustine of Hippo has been prominent for his teaching on peace. He says that as the peace of man is an orderly obedience to the eternal law of God, so the peace of God's city is "the perfect union of hearts, in the enjoyment of God and of one another in God" (*De Civitate Dei*, 19.13).

The idea of peace figures prominently in the Christian liturgy. "Peace be with you," "The peace of the Lord be always with you" are familiar liturgical greetings in the Latin rite. Before Holy Communion in the Latin Mass, it is the custom to give one another a sign of peace.

It is clear, therefore, that Christianity is deeply committed to peace. Toward the end of this book, some of the steps the Catholic Church has taken in the promotion of peace will be outlined.

JUDAISM ON PEACE

Judaism brings the *shalom* of God to people who follow his way. It inculcates love, truth, and obedience to the commandments of God. Peace is God's gift to his people. Aaron was instructed to bless the people with the following prayer: "May the Lord uncover his face to you and bring you peace" (Nm 6:26).

Peace is a mark of the messianic kingdom where righteousness and peace embrace each other (cf. Ps 85:10). All the nations will stream to the mountain of the Lord where he will teach them his ways. There will be no war. The peoples "will hammer their swords into plowshares, their spears into sickles. Nation will not lift sword against nation, there will be no more training for war" (Is 2:4). The prophet Micah beautifully adds: "Each man will sit under his vine and his fig tree, with no one to trouble him" (Mi 4:4). The biblical people of Israel are to look forward to the reign of the ideal Davidic king, the Prince of Peace, who will install a wide dominion in a peace that has no end (cf. Is 9:6–7).

For the Jews, *shalom* refers to both material and spiritual elements. God speaks of peace to his people. Righteousness and peace embrace. The land yields its fruit. People are to avoid the evils of deceit and uncontrolled desire. False prophets should not deceive the people by saying "Peace, peace," when there is no peace (cf. Jer 6:14). Not only is there no external danger in the genuine concept of *shalom* (and this is already much, especially in the days of the prophet Jeremiah), but peace includes an ideal state of happiness in which individual and nation prosper and social harmony reigns.

The Talmud states: "The whole Torah [i.e., the whole of Judaism] is for the sake of the ways of peace" (*Tractate Gittin*, 59B).

The great Spanish Jew, Moses Maimonides (1135–1204), in his *Code of Jewish Practice*, the *Yad Hahazakah*, in the section of the Laws of Kings, X, 11, writes: "Our sages commanded us to visit the sick even of heathens and to bury their dead with the dead of Israel for the sake of 'the ways of peace,' for behold it is stated, 'and his mercies are extended to *all* his creatures' (Psalm 145:9) and it is stated, 'Torah's ways are pleasant ways and all her paths are peace'" (Proverbs 3:17).

On this and similar texts of Maimonides, Rabbi David Rosen comments: "Respect and responsibility toward the other are described in Jewish Tradition as 'the ways of peace.' In other words, if we really care about peace, we will behave with respect and compassion to all human beings, regardless of their race or creed" (David Rosen, *The Role of Religion in the Pursuit of Peace*, in *Religion and Violence, Religion and Peace*, ed. by Joseph H. Ehrenkranz and D. Coppola, Fairfield, Connecticut, 2000, p. 121).

At the Assisi World Day of Prayer for Peace in 1986, Rabbi Elio Toaff, Chief Rabbi of Rome, led the Jewish Prayer with the following opening words: "Our God in heaven, the Lord of Peace, will have compassion and mercy upon us and upon the peoples of the earth who implore his mercy and his compassion, asking for peace, seeking peace."

ISLAM ON PEACE

In Islam, "peace," *salām*, is one of the Ninety-nine Beautiful Names of God. When Muslims greet one another, in prayer as in daily life, they offer to their neighbor this divine quality by saying *Al-salām 'alaykum* (Peace be upon you).

God summons people to the "Abode of Peace" (*dār al-salām*) both in this life and in the next (Q 10:26). The Qur'an is believed to have come down "on the Night of Power," and "Peace it is, till the rising of dawn" (Q 97:5).

The peace greeting, *al-salām 'alaykum*, is believed to be

that given to the blessed when they enter paradise. The common salutation in the Islamic world is never omitted by a devout Muslim after the mention of the name of Muhammad or of earlier prophets like Noah, Abraham, Moses, and Jesus.

"In the Name of God, the Merciful, the Compassionate": so begins the Qur'an. The verse is repeated at the beginning of every one of the 114 Surah (chapter) except Surah 9. Muslims often start a prayer or speech with this exclamation. Mercy, compassion, and peace are familiar concepts in the Qur'an.

The person who is given the peace greeting is expected to reciprocate and return the greeting with an additional blessing according to the Qur'anic advice: "And when you are greeted with a greeting, greet with a fairer than it, or return it" (Q 4:86). So Muslims respond to *al-salām 'alaykum* by saying *wa-'alaykum al-salām wa-rahmat Allah wa-barakātuhu* (And on you be peace and the mercy of God and his blessings).

Islamic tradition has it that once someone asked Muhammad: "O Prophet, give me a masterly piece of advice that will enable me to manage all the affairs of my life." He got the reply: "Don't be angry." This is very healthy advice to build for peace. Another tradition reports Muhammad as saying: "Don't wish for confrontation with your enemy, instead, always ask for peace from God."

The Qur'an states that if a person repays evil with

good, that person will win the enemy over to become a friend: "Not equal are the good deed and the evil deed. Repel with that which is fairer and behold, he between whom and thee there is enmity shall be as if he were a loyal friend" (Q 41:34).

Jihād is taken popularly to mean holy war. But the experts tell us that this is not the original Islamic sense of the term. The term generally means endeavor, striving, struggle. It denotes effort toward a commendable aim. In religious contexts it can mean the struggle against one's evil inclinations, or efforts toward the moral uplift of society or toward the spread of Islam. This last undertaking can be peaceful (*jihād* of the tongue, or *jihād* of the pen), or it can involve the use of force (*jihād* of the sword) as mentioned in Surah 2:189: "Fight them, till there is no persecution and the religion is God's; then if they give over, there shall be no enmity save for evildoers." Islamic pious and mystical circles put the emphasis on spiritual and moral *jihād* and they call this the "greater *Jihād*" (cf. Rudolph Peters, *Jihād*, in M. Eliade, *The Encyclopedia of Religion*, 8, pp. 88–91).

The Qur'an says that on the day of judgment, God will say to the faithful person: "O soul at peace, return unto thy Lord" (Q 89:28). Islam sees paradise as the divine haven of peace. But to reach there, people must obey God on earth. An Islamic saying has it: "God will guide men to peace. If they will heed him, he will lead them from the darkness of war to the light of peace."

HINDUISM ON PEACE

Hinduism sets high value on peace. The Sanskrit word often used for "peace" is *śāntih*. Many Hindu texts open with the sacred syllable *om*, followed by a threefold repetition of *śāntih* for invocation and meditation. The peace invoked in the texts refers to tranquillity, quiet, calmness of mind, absence of passion, aversion of pain, and indifference to objects of pleasure and pain (cf. G. Parrinder, *Peace*, in M. Eliade, *The Encyclopedia of Religion*, 11, p. 223).

Two Hindu sayings summarize the attitude of Hinduism toward peace: "Without meditation, where is peace? Without peace, where is happiness?" "If one would find happiness and security, one must seek for peace."

BUDDHISM ON PEACE

Suffering is the point of departure and indeed the foundation of all Buddhist teaching. Buddhism can indeed be said to be a doctrine that preaches the liberation of humanity from suffering. The teaching of the Buddha is summarized in the four Noble Truths, all with reference to suffering, regarding its existence, its cause, its end, and how to be free from it and reach *nirvana*.

The first truth, the reality on suffering, says that everything is suffering: birth, sickness, old age, union with an unloved person, separation from a loved one, not getting what one wants; in short, the five material and spiritual elements together with attachment are suffering. Every happiness or joy in this world, marked as it is by instability and transience, is already suffering. The Buddha says that during our existence we have shed more tears than the water contained in the four oceans (cf. *Samyuttanikâya* II, 180).

The Buddha says that the cause of suffering is attachment. This can take the form of longing or thirst for things, or an egoistical clinging to them. It can lead to the fear of loss. This is the second truth about suffering.

The third truth about suffering refers to its end or conclusion, the annihilation of attachment-thirst, of hatred, and of error is *nirvana*, the state of holiness. *Nirvana* (exit, escape) is the suppression of the fire of attachment-thirst and of the passions. Buddhist ascetism aims at reaching the *nirvana* (extinction) of self and the purification of self. The Buddhist saint is the one who has realized an emptying and denial of self and passions.

Nirvana can be reached in this world by destroying selfish attachment, which is the root of all suffering, but it is obtained in a definitive way only after death. This *nirvana*, because of the absolute absence of suffering in it, is called Ineffable Peace, Perfect Calm, Supreme Beatitude, or Full Happiness.

In the fourth truth, the Buddha indicates the way that leads to *nirvana*. The eightfold way to righteousness is as follows: right vision, right thought, right word, right action, right life, right effort, right attention, and right meditation.

In Buddhism, therefore, peace (*sāntih*) is identified with

nirvana and with the state of holiness (*arhattva*) that becomes a state of undisturbed tranquillity (*upeksā*). In this sense, peace is the final end of Buddhism. According to the teaching of Buddha, peace is realized negatively through the practice of nonviolence (*ahisā*) and positively through the perfection of benevolence-compassion (*maitrī-karunā*) toward all living beings.

It is recorded that the famous Indian ruler, the Buddhist emperor Aśoka, in the third century B.C., after thousands of people had been killed in his war against the Kalingas, felt remorse, renounced war, sought reconciliation, and wished that all beings should be unharmed, self-controlled, calm in mind, and gentle. Fighting was forbidden. So was all killing of animals for food or sacrifice (cf. G. Parrinder, op. cit., p. 223).

JAINISM ON PEACE

Founded in the sixth century B.C. by a contemporary of Buddha in India, Jainism shares with Buddhism the absence of belief in a personal God and of reference or prayer to him, although the two traditions do not deny God.

The ultimate goal of life for Jains consists in seeking liberation and purification of soul through rigorous moral discipline such as nonviolence toward all (therefore, strict vegetarian diet) and willing acceptance of death. The way to *nirvana* (a passive state of beatitude) is through right faith, right knowledge, and right conduct. The way to obtain these is the practice of austerity, mortification, and asceticism; for example, through forgiveness, humility, simplicity, absence of greed, fasting, control of mind, body, and speech, honesty, external and internal purity, chastity and detachment from people and property (cf. Pont. Council for Interreligious Dialogue, *Journeying Together*, Rome 1999, pp. 43–44).

The reader can see that this is truly a recipe for peace.

TRADITIONAL RELIGIONS ON PEACE

These religions are known in Africa as African traditional religion, in Asia as Tribal religion, in Australia as Aboriginal religion, and in America as Native American religion. While there is no strict or organizational unity among these religious traditions, they are generally marked by belief in one God, in spirits good and bad, and in ancestors, with due worship offered in varying degrees to the three gradations of superior beings.

Traditional religions regard God, the Great Spirit, as the Creator of the world and the lesser spirits and the ancestors as looking after the details of human existence such as marriage, the family, society relationships, observance of customs, and agricultural life. People are to follow the laws of these superior powers in all these sectors of life if they are to live in peace and tranquillity. Sacrifices of expiation are to be offered by people who commit abominations or major violations of customs. If there is tension, unrest or war, it is thought to be because some people have violated the customary laws.

The morning prayer of the father for his household, of the chief or king for his people or clan during a festival, or of the priest at the shrine of a spirit, always includes an intercession for peace and quiet in the family, in the village, and in the wider society.

OTHER RELIGIONS ON PEACE

Other religions also speak about peace. Here, to conclude, are a few further quotations.

Sikhism: "By saturating my mind, the true Name has satisfied all my longings, and given me peace and happiness." "Only in the Name of the Lord do we find our peace."

Zoroastrianism: "All men and women should mutually love one another and live in peace as brothers and sisters, bound by the indestructible hand of Humanity." "I will sacrifice to peace, whose breath is friendly."

Taoism: "The good ruler seeks peace and not war, and he rules by persuasion rather than by force."

Shintoism: "The earth shall be free from trouble and we shall live in peace under the protection of the divine."

Baha'i: "Today there is no greater glory for man than that of service in the cause of the 'Most Great Peace.'" "War is death while Peace is life."

Confucianism: "Seek to be in harmony with all your neighbors . . . live in peace with your brethren."

It can therefore be concluded that the various religions of the world are all in favor of peace. And most people in the world are followers of one or another religion. Why then is there so much tension, violence, and even war in the world? Do the religions have any hand in this? This is a serious question that must now engage our attention.

THREE

Do Religions Cause War?

THE CASE AGAINST RELIGION

Some people argue that in the seeking of harmony and peace, the religions of the world may be part of the problem rather than part of the solution. Some even say that along the corridors of history, religions have caused tension, violence, or war, or exacerbated them. For such people, discussion on interreligious collaboration for the promotion of peace is so much pious and unrealistic talk, if not purely wasted time. They therefore suggest that religions should be excluded in considerations for peace building. Some of their arguments are the following.

A religion offers a worldview to a particular community and thereby segregates it from the rest of humanity. It is thus a fertile origin for prejudices, unilateral vision, intolerance, and even antagonism. They quote the vehemence with which some religious views can be held, together with the readiness of some religious people to die for their beliefs.

They argue that religious differences have often been, and continue to be, a major cause of conflict, and that people in the name of one religion or another have sometimes brought discord, distrust, tension, pain, conflict, and suffering to one another and to the wider world. They quote as examples the Crusades waged by Christians in the Middle Ages and the Wars of Conquest or "Holy Wars" waged by Muslims even in our times.

The activities of religious extremists, called "fundamentalists" by some people, are seen as a proof that the promotion of peace does not come from religions. These extremists, no matter how well intentioned, do not hesitate to resort to repression, blackmail, harassment, kidnapping, violence, and even killing of fellow human beings—all in the name of what they regard as a return to the genuine state of their particular religion. And when their fundamentalist tendencies are used to feed nationalist sentiments, the results become more negative still.

There is a further argument against religions' making a positive contribution to harmony and peace. It has been noted that in some cases of ethnic, racial, or economic conflict, religion has served to fuel intolerance and discrimination. Sometimes twisted religious considerations have been mixed with ethnic resentments and unhealed historical memories to generate or promote tension, violence, and actual killing of fellow human beings.

For all such reasons, the doubters say that the religions of the world have a case to answer and that they should not be parading themselves as promoters of peace.

WHAT GENUINE RELIGION IS ALL ABOUT

Let us open the case for the defense on behalf of religions by examining what a genuine religion is all about. True religion is concerned primarily with the worship of God, which includes adoration, praise, thanksgiving, love, and the making of supplications. Love of God, as said earlier, necessarily includes, and is closely followed by, love of neighbor. "Anyone who says, 'I love God' and hates his brother, is a liar," St. John tells us, "since a man who does not love the brother that he can see cannot love God, whom he has never seen" (1 Jn 4:20). The promotion of hatred, violence, and war is the opposite of what true religion is all about. It has already been seen how the Golden Rule—Do to others as you would like them to do to you—is part of the patrimony of most religions.

A true believer is known by love of neighbor, by the readiness to admit guilt where there has been any wrong done and to ask for forgiveness, by openness to reconciliation, and by the positive promotion of solidarity among peoples, cultures, and religions. The beneficial influence of religion on social life is undoubted. Many societies, including those hitherto accustomed to a sharp separation between religious and state affairs, are beginning more and more to appreciate the contribution of the religions in various areas of social life: education, health, conflict prevention or resolution, social healing and reconciliation after conflict, work for refugees, help to the poor so that they can improve their level of life, and all-around human development projects. All this is contributory to peace.

RELIGION CONDEMNS VIOLENCE

To do violence to an innocent person is the opposite of love for that person. A religion that teaches violence or war is to that extent a travesty, a negation of what religion is about. Speaking to delegates to the World Conference on Religion and Peace, Pope John Paul II declared: "Religion is not, and must not become, a pretext for conflict, particularly when religious, cultural, and ethnic identity coincide. In recent days, sadly, I have had reason to affirm once more that: 'No one can consider himself faithful to the great and merciful God who in the name of the same God dares to kill his brother' (General Audience, Oct. 26, 1994). Religion and Peace go together: to wage war in the name of religion is a blatant contradiction. I hope that you will be able, during your Conference, to find ways to spread this profound conviction" (Address on Nov. 4, 1994, n.2, in *L'Osser. Rom.*, Weekly Eng. Ed., Nov. 16, 1994, p. 2)

In his message to the Millennium World Peace Summit

of Religious and Spiritual Leaders, held in the United Nations plenary assembly hall on August 29, 2000, the Pope returned to the same theme. He told the one thousand assembled participants that their assembly was "an exceptional opportunity to make it abundantly clear that the only religion worthy of the name is the religion that leads to peace and that true religion is mocked when it is tied to conflict and violence." Indeed, that assembly in its final document, entitled "Commitment to Global Peace," condemned all violence committed in the name of religion.

Other assemblies have done likewise. Earlier the UNESCO Berne Declaration of November 26, 1992, had stated that "a crime committed in the name of religion is a crime against religion"; and the Bosphorus Declaration of February 9, 1994, insisted: "We reject the concept that it is possible to justify one's actions in any armed conflict in the name of God."

CONFLICTS CAN HAVE MULTIPLE CAUSES

When tensions or conflicts break out between people in such places as the Sudan, some northern States in Nigeria, Ivory Coast, India, Indonesia, parts of the Middle East, Bosnia and Herzegovina, and even Northern Ireland, some commentators oversimplify matters by saying that the conflicts are caused by religion. This is often true only in part. There may well be other causes: ethnic rivalry, racial tensions, quarrels over land, and economic struggles. There may also be the burden of history, unhealed memories of past injustices, whether these be real or merely perceived. All these grievances may be smoldering below the surface.

Nor should it be forgotten that religion is sometimes used by unscrupulous politicians for their own ends. Dissensions are created, so that political points can be made. When religion has thus been abused and exploited, people turn around and blame the religion. But this would only be to hide the real motivations that explain the outbursts of violence, economically oppressive measures, massacres, so-called ethnic cleansing, or other acts of injustice that fallen human nature is all too prone to perpetrate.

It follows that believers must not allow themselves to be recruited in acts of violence by people who have hidden agendas. To the extent to which a person hates others and adopts violent measures against them, to that extent that person is not a good member of any genuine religion.

Let me illustrate by one example. Some years back, a friend wrote our office from one city that I prefer not to name. There had been interreligious violence there. He told us that there was a systematic campaign to spread hatred against people of the other religion. He emphasized that the ordinary people of the two religious communities live in peace in harmony, but that it is the politicians and thugs who promote the violence. This is the sort of abuse of religion that all true religious leaders have to strive to avoid.

Generally, action leading to tension, violence, or war can be traced to pride, intolerance, the egoism of the individual or the group, greed, envy, and desire for revenge. It is precisely such situations that religion is called upon to heal, taking care not to become their victim or, worse still, their tool. "Happy are the peacemakers, for they will be called children of God" (Mt 5:9).

NEED FOR SOUL-SEARCHING
AMONG BELIEVERS

The above explanations have not entirely solved the vexed queston of whether religions contribute to violence. People of the various religions must be willing to look deeper into the matter, into the historical record of their religions and into their own personal consciences.

It is an accepted fact that a religion creates a common philosophy of life among its followers. They tend to have a similar outlook on the major problems that accompany or torment human existence on earth, such as the existence of God and people's relationship with him, the cause and meaning of suffering and death, the determination of moral good or evil, matters touching marriage and the family, and the relationship between religion and public affairs.

By the fact that religion unites people in a faith community, it can also inadvertently separate them from other groups if care is not taken. This is more likely to happen where religious adherence is along lines of race, political power, social class, or material wealth.

Moreover, tension can arise when a group perceives itself as threatened, even when that group is in the wrong. Even the most enlightened and peaceful religious group can inadvertently heighten tension because it resists what it sees as a situation of injustice. If a religious group opposes apartheid, racism, the denial of civil rights for underprivileged citizens, slavery, child labor, the recruitment of child soldiers, and prostitution especially by entrapped children and women, it is to be expected that such a pursuit of justice and fair play is likely to arouse the hostility of those who are profiting from the situations named above. In this sense, we cannot blame Our Lord Jesus Christ if his preaching aroused the envy and hostility of the Scribes and Pharisees and other Jewish leaders who felt threatened by his Gospel of liberation, love for everyone, humility, truth, and service.

People of religions, however, should go carefully and not be too quick to declare themselves innocent and other people guilty of any ensuing violence. The desire of the originators of the Crusades, for example, may have been blameless and religiously acceptable: to get back the Holy Places sanctified by the life, suffering, and death of Jesus Christ. But that does not mean that everything de facto done by the crusaders is to be approved. A Muslim may be blameless in desiring to share his religion with others. But it is quite another matter what means he uses to spread that conviction. Force, violence, destruction, and conquest cannot be approved.

Every religion, especially the major ones, should also undertake some form of examination of conscience. How has it fared all through the centuries? How has it treated people of other religious convictions who are a minority where it is in the majority? Does it accept the principle that every human being should be free from coercion in religious matters, including the possibility of a change of religious adherence? Has it always condemned the use of violence? Has it upheld human rights? What does it teach about religion and public life especially in view of growing religious plurality in the world, and at the same time the inroads of secularism, materialism, hedonism, and even atheism? What has it contributed to local and world peace? If mistakes have been made by members of that religion now or in the past, is that religion ready to accept these facts, to repent, to apologize, and to try to turn over a new leaf?

Mr. Kofi Annan, the Secretary-General of the United Nations, reflecting on the interplay of forces, motivations, and human weakness in this complicated matter, said to the assembly of the Millennium World Peace Summit of Religious and Spiritual Leaders already mentioned: "Religion is frequently equated with light. But we all know that the practice of religion can have its dark side, too. Religious extremism has too often oppressed or discriminated against women and minorities. Religion has often been yoked to nationalism, stoking the flames of violent conflict and setting group against group. Religious leaders have not always spoken out when their voices could have helped combat hatred and persecution or could have roused people from indifference. Religion is not itself to blame: as I have often said, the problem is usually not with the faith, but with the faithful."

RESPONSIBILITY OF
RELIGIOUS LEADERS

The foregoing considerations show that the role of religious leaders is important. They help to form, motivate, and conscientize their coreligionists on what to do, or not to do, so that each religion will always promote peace and not tension, violence, or war.

∽ Religious plurality is a growing fact in the world today. All the factors of modern life—communications, ease of travel, interlinking economies, international organizations—indicate that the meeting of peoples, cultures, and religions will continue to move forward. Many Muslim Turks live in Germany and Holland. Many Christian Filipinos live in Saudi Arabia and the Emirates. Hindus have settled in England. Buddhists have monasteries in Switzerland. There is no part of the world today that is not religiously pluralistic in nature.

∽ The fact of religious plurality should be accepted, especially by religious leaders who should help and orient their coreligionists to accept and live with this fact. When interdependence is not just tolerated but is accepted and lived, it becomes the high moral value of solidarity.

⥽ Religious leaders have also to admit that they have not always all lived in accordance with the high ideals that they preach. Repentance, mutual forgiveness, and reconciliation are needed on all sides.

⥽ Many religions have internal conflicts that damage their unity. The leaders should seek peaceful solutions to the issues on which there is division. Internal unity will help promote good relations with other believers.

⥽ The followers of the various religions have also to be helped to identify the different elements that can contribute to a particular conflict: ethnic, economic, political, historical, and religious. The UNESCO Barcelona Declaration of December 18, 1994, made this careful distinction: "We will remain mindful that our religions must not identify themselves with political, economic, or social powers, so as to remain free to work for justice and peace. We will not forget that confessional political regimes do serious harm to religious values as well as society. We should distinguish fanaticism from religious zeal" (in the *Istanbul Symposium Working Document,* p. 141).

⥽ For the achievement of social cohesion the kind of leadership that people receive in their religious community is of considerable importance. While religious leaders need not be held responsible for every action of their core-ligionists, it is nevertheless true that the inspirational role of the leaders in the various religions does influence society. Religion offers deep-seated motivations for which people are prepared to make sacrifices, not excluding life itself, whereas very few people would be prepared to lay down their lives for the sake of mathematics or geography. Therefore the considerations made above regarding acceptance of others, respect for their conscience, and willingness to work with them, do imply obligations on religious leaders to inculcate the same by word and example.

 &em; Believers in the various religions realize that their religions must show themselves in works of justice, respect for human rights, development, human promotion, and peace. Religion would evaporate into arid philosophy if it did not grapple with concrete situations that people face in their ordinary day-to-day living.

 &em; Leaders of various religious traditions have the necessary role of striving to encourage interreligious cooperation in works of human promotion. While a few people are enough to cause tension, confusion, and destruction, the cooperation of all is needed in order to promote lasting development, justice, and peace. There are problems and challenges that do not respect religious frontiers: corruption in public life, wrong attitude to work or to the good of the country, and discrimination against people because of their color, ethnic background, or sex. There are development questions that no one religious community can solve single-handedly: uncontrolled urbanization, the growing gap between the rich and the poor, runaway inflation. All these and similar challenges are best faced when all believers, drawing from the highest ideals of their respective religions, work together to find adequate solutions. The role of their leaders in encouraging such cooperation is important.

On the African continent, many cases of civil tension and violence are due to political instability, the difficulty of getting democratic constitutions to work, the attitude of politicians who find it hard to accept defeat in an election, or the sheer challenge of building a modern state out of many peoples of varying ethnic backgrounds thrown together because boundaries were arbitrarily fixed by the colonial powers. In all such situations, a positive contribution can be made by wise religious leaders. They can help to promote harmony, to go through a process of social change successfully, and to establish a tradition of peaceful and smooth political transfer of power (cf. Statement of Symposium on the Role of Religious Leaders in Peacemaking and Social Change in Africa, in *Weltkirche* 8/1993, pp. 231–235).

The U. N. Secretary General encouraged religious leaders in the speech already quoted: "I humbly suggest that today's meeting is also an opportunity for religious, spiritual, and political leaders, as well as their followers, to look within, and to consider what they can do to promote justice, equality, reconciliation, and peace. Men and women of faith are a strong influence on group and individual conduct. As teachers and guides, you can be powerful agents of change. You can inspire people to new levels of commitment and public service. You can help bridge the chasms of ignorance, fear, and misunderstanding. You can set an example of interfaith dialogue and cooperation."

It is therefore certain that religions can help promote peace. And they should. A necessary requirement is that everyone, especially religious leaders, does his or her part.

Seeing, however, that religion and culture are closely related, it is useful to examine how religions and cultures can contribute to harmony and peace rather than to tension and war. This will be the topic for the next chapter.

FOUR

Religions and Cultures as Help or Hindrance to Peace

Rather close to our reflection in the last chapter is a consideration of the extent to which cultural differences, almost always heavily influenced by one religion or another, do help toward peace promotion or, on the contrary, hinder it.

RELIGION AND CULTURE

When we think of the culture of a people, our thoughts go to how they have developed and humanized their ways of living, their artistic expressions, their mentality and institutions, their literature, science, and technology. Religion is an important dimension of each people's culture. In a way, religion can be called the transcendent dimension of culture. It shows how people relate to God, or the Absolute Being, or the Great Spirit, or simply the divine. This will then be reflected in the way they live their life in society. Where one religion is that of the majority of the people, this religion generally so influences the culture that it is at times difficult to say where culture finishes and religion begins.

To understand a people, it is important therefore to understand its culture and its religion.

MEETING OF RELIGIONS AND CULTURES TODAY

For many reasons the world map today presents us with people from different religions, cultures, and civilizations living side by side. Accelerated migration, relative ease of jet travel, globalization of industrial concerns, and need to travel because of educational, economic, cultural, or political considerations, are some of the reasons.

Every religion contributes something to the culture of the people who practice it. Sometimes several religious traditions coexist within the same cultural framework. At other times one major religion finds expression in a particular culture. Thus Christianity, Islam, Hinduism, and Confucianism have all been associated with major civilizations. But Buddhism and the Traditional Religions have also left their imprint. Indeed, it is difficult to find a religion that has not somehow influenced culture.

For illustration, let us consider Europe and how Christianity has contributed to its culture.

CONTRIBUTION OF CHRISTIANITY TO EUROPEAN CULTURE

Christianity began, as we know, in Asia, in Palestine, in West Asia, which many are accustomed to call the Middle East. But in the earlier days of its spread, Christianity came to Europe (cf. Acts 16:10), met Greek philosophy and Roman law, and inculturated itself.

European culture cannot be properly understood if the contribution that Christianity has made to Europe is not taken into consideration. Although not all the people in this continent are Christians, and not all those who are may be truly living according to their faith, Christianity has given Europe some of its finest cultural values.

Faith in God as Creator and Providence has influenced family life and language and given a sense of respect for what is sacred to God.

The Christian belief in the Son of God taking on human nature and suffering and dying for all men and women, is an important background to the European value of respect for the dignity of every human being. That Christ calls himself our brother and has instituted his Church to which everyone is offered membership, is an important Christian consideration for treating others as brothers and sisters.

[43]

Architecture, art, and literature in Europe cannot be understood without reference to Christianity, which nourished it and gave it its symbols. Yet the influence of Christianity is not limited to the domain of art.

The ideas that today are taken for granted in a democratic society: the rule of law, the equality of people before the law, the rights of women, the rights of minorities, and, in general, the fundamental human rights, are all fruits of the Christian tree planted long ago. They may have been given an impulse by the French Revolution, which was largely opposed to the Church. Yet the Christian roots lay deep.

Today the social doctrine of the Church spells out in clearer terms the Christian understanding of such important matters as the sacredness of life from conception to natural death, the fundamental role of the family founded on the marriage of man and woman, the rights of workers and of their employers, the responsibilities of the rich and the duty of solidarity, and civil authority understood as service and not as domination. Although everyone in Europe has not been one hundred percent faithful to these values, there is no doubt that the past two thousand years have seen these values nourished and taken seriously by European culture. This is not to deny that some signs of decadence are now appearing. But the Christian matrix is undoubted.

It should be noted that in Europe the Jews were present before the arrival of Christianity. And today in Europe we have not only Christians and Jews, but also Muslims, Hindus, Buddhists, Sikhs, Baha'i, Jains, and other believers. Account has also to be taken of those who are religiously indifferent or even nonbelievers. There are others who adhere to new religious movements in an effort to give expression to their religious sentiment.

A further factor is constituted by the racial and cultural differences that people show. These differences can be observed easily, merely by watching people's faces or by paying attention to the way they dress.

Now the question arises: What contribution do religions and cultures make to peace in such religiously and culturally pluralist societies?

CHALLENGES TO BE FACED

Multiculturality and religious plurality offer challenges and opportunities that have to be faced if peace is to be constructed. Dialogue among cultures and traditions, says Pope John Paul II, "is the obligatory path to the building of a reconciled world, a world able to look with serenity to its own future" (*Message for World Day of Peace*, 2001, n. 3). Indeed the United Nations Organization declared the year 2001 the "International Year of Dialogue Among Civilizations."

A person finds a needed form of self-expression and a formula for growth by proper insertion into his or her own culture. Family, social groups, thought patterns, language, school, religion, and social life in general—all go to help that person integrate into a definite culture.

People should accept the fact that every culture, since it is a typically human reality and also historically conditioned, will necessarily have its strong points and its weak points. Each culture has to accept that it has limitations. The human race is bigger, wider, and richer than any one culture.

It follows that exchange among cultures, give and take, healthy encounter—in short, dialogue—is an intrinsic demand of human nature itself, as well as of culture. Cultural differences can become a source of misunderstanding between peoples and can occasion or cause tension and conflict. But it does not have to be so. It is for wise human beings to see that the meeting of cultures and religions may lead to harmony rather than result in a clash.

This is easier said than done. Some considerations are offered here that can be of help in this difficult task.

VALUES THAT APPEAL TO MOST RELIGIONS AND CULTURES

There are some values, human, spiritual, and religious, that strike a positive chord in the hearts of most religious people and are to be found in most cultures.

The need to accept other human beings as brothers and sisters, rather than to treat them as enemies or threats, in the journey of life, is understood across religious and cultural frontiers. Such acceptance is proved by an attitude of respect toward other people, with their differences, both religious and cultural. It is promoted by a willingness to listen, to receive, to give, to share. Most people understand what is meant by a closed attitude of self-sufficiency as opposed to ready acceptance of interdependence among people and among peoples. Solidarity or mutual sharing and building one another up in the pilgrimage that is life, is a moral virtue appreciated by all normal people and cultures.

Social, cultural, and religious respect for marriage, the family, the child, and human life in its various stages of development, is a healthy element in cultures and religions that have not taken the downward road to decadence.

The religious attitude illustrated by a willingness to acknowledge fault where there has been any, to repent, to ask and give forgiveness, and to seek reconciliation, is something truly precious that appeals to the human heart. Something similar could be said about such virtues as honesty in speech and work, gratitude to benefactors, hospitality to visitors (many peoples and cultures love to refer to their "traditional hospitality"), and gratuitous love shown to the poor and needy.

Most people in the various religions and cultures may not live these ideals in their purest and highest forms. But at least they appreciate them. And this is an important element in the contribution of religions and cultures to the building of peace.

There are some challenges that, especially in the world today, do not spare any religion or culture but that rather would appear to call on them to close ranks and seek together viable solutions to these problems.

There is first the fact of multiculturality and religious plurality, especially in the larger modern cities. Can the followers of different religions and people belonging to different cultures pretend that they do not notice the presence of others?

The pressing problems of uncontrolled urbanization, unemployment especially in today's monster cities, the crushing poverty of huge populations who live at the fringes of the cities in unworthy human situations, and the painful phenomenon of roaming street children, cannot leave believers unconcerned.

Religions and civilizations are worried by the inroads of secularism, hedonism, consumerism, and a use-and-throw-away mentality into some of their most cherished patrimonies. Although television, the electronic media, and the press can do much good, they can also, for instance, desacralize and banalize marriage and the family. They can present an unreal world out of the reach of most people. The challenge is to use the modern communications media well in order to build a solid base for peace.

This is the positive attitude to assume. It does not help merely to condemn their abuses.

The sense of community that has sustained most individuals in their religious and cultural identity is harder to maintain when the person leaves the village for the big city. There the individual can feel alone even in a population of a million. A lonely, unemployed, or hungry person is a ready tool for a wild revolutionary who promises a happy future after a swift, violent operation. What response have the religions to this?

The temptation to use violent means—armed robbery, terrorism, assassination, rioting, or violent revolution—is never to be totally excluded where people are languishing under bad government, corruption, poverty, oppression, repression, or even just unemployment and the effects of a poor economy. Here is another challenge for all who hold dearly the finer elements of their religion and culture.

RELIGIONS SHOULD EDUCATE
PEOPLE IN BASIC VIRTUES

To meet these challenges and prevent a clash between people of varying religious and cultural backgrounds, the religions of the world should make a great effort to educate their followers in the basic virtues that can help peace building.

If we examine religions carefully, we can observe that

the basis for the high ideals of justice, peace, and unity are found at their very heart. Indeed, most religions regard as self-evident that God is the Creator of all human beings, that human nature is the same in all men and women, that all share the desire to love, to be loved, and to attain happiness, and that God is the final destiny of man, because he is the only one who can give complete and never-ending fulfillment to the human heart. Moreover, genuine religion teaches men and women that they are social beings who can flourish best in societies where mutual acceptance and respect and a desire for collaboration are to be found.

The role of religion in the advancement of justice, peace, and unity can also be seen from the consideration that religion has the power to appeal to some of the deepest and most powerful motives for human action. For religious motives, for example, people are ready to acknowledge and confess their faults, to repent and ask forgiveness, to resolve to do better in future, to forgive and to seek reconciliation with those who have hurt them. For the sake of religion, people are prepared to resist temptations to revenge and to egoism, whether of the individual or of the group, linguistic, ethnic, religious, or otherwise. For the sake of religion, people are even ready to lay down their lives for others, as Jesus himself taught us by word and example: "A man can have no greater love than to lay down his life for his friends" (Jn 15:13). And Jesus laid down his life even for those who did not love him.

It is therefore clear that religion can contribute to justice, peace, and unity. Indeed, the various religions have a duty to do so, unless they want to marginalize themselves into interesting relics of bygone days, or into fossilized institutions rather than ways of life very relevant to the world today.

WHILE RESPECTING RELIGIOUS AND CULTURAL IDENTITIES

The religious and cultural harmony and collaboration that is being advocated here should not be interpreted to mean a loss of one's identity. Let us examine first how this applies to interreligious contacts and then how it is to be verified in intercultural relations.

Interreligious dialogue is a sincere meeting of a person deeply convinced of his own faith, with a believer in another religion. It presupposes peaceful possession of one's religious identity card, and membership in such good standing in one's religious community that one can be named an ambassador of that community.

Interreligious dialogue is therefore not for religious indifferentists, not for those who are problem children in their faith community, not for academicians who entertain doubt about some fundamental articles of their own faith, nor for religious iconoclasts who have already shattered sacred statues and shaken some of the pillars on which their religion is built. It would be a mistake to allow such doubters into the arena of interreligious dialogue. A country does not appoint as its ambassador a citizen whose loyalty is suspect.

It is instructive that the Second Vatican Council, which had such a clear self-image of what the Church is and of the universal mission entrusted to her by Christ (cf. LG, AG), is also the Council that insisted that Catholics should meet other believers and "in witness of Christian faith and life, acknowledge, preserve, and promote the spiritual and moral goods found among these men, as well as the values in their society and culture" (*Nostra Aetate*, 2).

In the effort of people of one culture to meet those of another, care is to be taken not to deprive oneself of one's cultural identity. Enrichment must not be interpreted to mean emptying and replacing. While it is unrealistic and opposed to harmonious living that one culture would resist every beneficial influence from any other culture, "no less perilous is the slavish conformity of cultures," says Pope John Paul II (*Message for World Day of Peace*, 2001, n. 9). The Pope gives as an example of this mistake the temptation to copy some aspects of Western or European culture that have detached themselves from their Christian origins. Such are cultural patterns marked by secularism (or living as if God did not exist), practical atheism, radical individualism, and nihilism. Dressed up in impressive scientific and technical garb, these negative trends can do much damage in eroding precious patrimonies in other cultures. Discretion is therefore needed for one culture to meet another and become enriched by the encounter.

If the above objectives are to be attained, and if the dangers and risks are to be kept at bay, then education is necessary. It is part of what was, in an earlier chapter, said to be one of the duties of religious leaders.

If religious and cultural myopia is to be avoided, then people must be helped to combine regard for their religious and cultural identity with reasonable understanding of other religions and cultures. While one must be able to define one's place in the world with reference to religious and cultural patterns, respect for those who are different is needed, together with genuine appreciation of what they have that is noble, true, good, and elevating.

This openness need not lead to theological relativism or cultural confusion. One's religion should orient one to meet other religions with a critical sense. A Christian, for example, should never give up faith in the uniqueness of Jesus Christ as Son of God made man and Savior of all humanity, who founded his Church to share the Good News of salvation with all. So equipped, the Christian will remain open to admire whatever the Holy Spirit may have worked in other people or their religious rites or cultures. On the cultural level, a person properly inserted in his or her culture, can with the necessary discretion meet people of different cultural backgrounds.

We must therefore conclude that while religions and the cultures in which they exist and function can occasion, or cause, or exacerbate tension and conflict, they need not do so. They should not do so. They should positively contribute to harmony, collaboration, and peace. For this to happen, people must do their part. And the religions themselves have a special role. What in greater detail is this role with reference to inculcating attitudes? That is the topic for our next chapter.

FIVE

Religions Inculcating Attitudes for Peace

One of the most crucial ways in which the religions of the world can help build peace is through inculcating attitudes that lead to peace or to its preservation. Let us reflect from different angles on how religions can do this.

ACCEPTANCE OF THE FACT OF RELIGIOUS PLURALITY

If there is no peace and mutual acceptance among people of varying religious persuasions, then peace in the wider society will not be possible. But for interreligious peace, one of the primary requirements is that believers accept the fact of religious plurality in the world. There are not only Christians in the world (they make up 33 percent of humanity, of whom 18 percent are Catholics and 15 percent are other Christians). There are also Muslims, who comprise around 18 percent, Hindus, who form 13 percent and Buddhists, who are 7 percent of the world population. Moreover, there are Jews, Sikhs, Traditional or Tribal religionists, Jains, Zoroastrians, Taoists, and Chinese folk religionists (cf. D. Barrett, *World Christian Encyclopaedia*, Nairobi, 1982, pp. 6, 782–785).

It is not only that there are many religions in the world, but that people of different religious convictions now live and work side by side more than in any previous century in human history. Today England, while being traditionally a Christian country, has also Jews, Muslims, Hindus, Sikhs, and Buddhists living in the same neighborhoods. Saudi Arabia, while being the birthplace of Islam, has a large number of Christians and also some Hindus and Buddhists working in various capacities. Thailand is a majority Buddhist cultural area, but Christians and Muslims are not absent there. Nigeria is a country where African traditional religion has been the religious and cultural context of life, but Muslims and Christians are now becoming more numerous than the followers of the traditional religion. There is now hardly any country in the world where religious diversity is absent. Sometimes in the same family, more often in the same office, football team, political party, university faculty, or trade union, there are people who belong to differing religious persuasions.

The religions should teach and convince their followers to accept this fact and to learn to live with it.

From acceptance of the fact of religiously pluralistic societies, the followers of the various religions have to learn to
work together to promote peace. Peace has no religious
frontiers. There is no separate Christian peace, Muslim
peace, Hindu peace, or Buddhist peace. Religions have no
choice but to work together to promote peace. "Interreligious contacts, together with ecumenical dialogue," says
Pope John Paul II, "now seem to be obligatory paths, in
order to ensure that the many painful wounds inflicted
over the course of centuries will not be repeated, and indeed that any such wounds still remaining will soon be
healed" (*Message for World Day of Prayer for Peace*, 1992, n. 6).

To precipitate tension or war, a few people are enough.
To build peace and maintain it, the cooperation of all is
required. Believers in the various religions have to be helped
to overcome misunderstandings, stereotypes, caricatures,
and other prejudices, inherited or acquired. They should
together strive to make their voices heard in favor of peace
in councils of state, in the communications media, and in
the marketplace. All hands should be on deck to shape society in such a way that people live in peace and tranquillity.

In this work of conscientization, religions that have their
followers in many countries all around the world are particularly well placed to help. If one state were to go to war
against another, it would follow that the followers of such

religions would find themselves fighting their coreligionists. This should make them pause and ask themselves on which side is right, on which side is God. A universalist religion should help people to see one another, not as enemies, but as brothers and sisters across religious and national frontiers. This attitude is very positive for peace promotion.

CONVERT THE HUMAN HEART

War begins in people's hearts with pride, rancor, hatred, and desire for revenge, before it is translated into armaments, open violence, and wanton destruction. Therefore to construct peace, it is advisable first to seek a conversion of hearts. With hearts and minds changed from hatred and greed to love and a desire for reconciliation, the weapons will drop from angry and hating hands, and the cultivation of a culture of peace can begin.

Education for peace has therefore to start with the formation of consciences, with conversion of heart. Selfishness, immoderate desire of earthly goods that are destined for the use of all, appropriation of what belongs to another—dishonesty in thought and word and open violence are the beginnings of war. It would be a false start to presume that people will not have these weaknesses. All religions have a duty to join hands to educate the human heart in honesty, love, benevolence, compassion, solidarity, self-control, and especially respect for the rights of others,

A very useful foundation for such initiatives is joint

study and teaching by the various religions on the dignity of the human person created by God in his own image and likeness (cf. Gen 1:26). Consequent on this dignity are the fundamental rights of every human being, which derive from God the Creator. Specific ethical and religious values are needed in addition to economic, social, and juridical structures, in order to promote peace. Here is where the religions come in. Therefore Pope John Paul II says in his May 1, 1991, Encyclical Letter: "I am convinced that the various religions, now and in the future, will have a preeminent role in preserving peace and in building a society worthy of man" (*Centesimus Annus*, 60).

St. James already advised the early Christians to control their passions so that they would have peace: "Where do these wars and battles between yourselves first start? Isn't it precisely in the desires fighting inside your own selves? You want something and you haven't got it; so you are prepared to kill. You have an ambition that you cannot satisfy; so you fight to get your way by force" (Jas 4:1–2). Religions can usefully teach the same asceticism and moral code today.

CONSCIENTIZE FOR PEACE

Religions should make their followers more and more aware of the need to construct peace. While it is true that religious differences can aggravate conflicts if there is not good leadership available, it is also undeniable and easily verifiable that moral values and convictions shared by people of many religions can provide a basis for communities and nations to live together in peace and harmony. Here are some such convictions.

Force, violence, and war do not bring peace. A person can beat another person in a fight, and yet not have interior peace. A country can defeat its neighbor in three or four wars and yet be far from peace, unless of course one is talking of the peace of the cemetery, the peace between the dead and those who killed them. Valor, strength, and military superiority can sometimes be demonstrated by forgiveness and readiness for reconciliation, rather than by the use of brute force. Religions are in a good position to extol such a value.

Fear can be the background to many cases of tension and consequent aggression. Racism, anti-Semitism, hate crimes, so-called ethnic cleasing, extremism, and other such violent acts may have in their causes a fair dosage of fear. The religions should help people to analyze their fears and to seek positive and acceptable solutions based on justice and love of others.

All religions have to deal with education on the right attitude to violence. There is violence against groups because of social, religious, cultural, economic, or political considerations, especially when they are minorities. There is violence in the form of rigged political elections, unjust demonstrations, terrorism, and assassinations. And there is violence that erupts as full-fledged war: tribal, civil, international, or otherwise.

True religion teaches self-control and that one should battle against one's passions that tend toward evil, but not battle against one's neighbor. Violence is not overcome by further violence. Hatred must be overcome by love, by conversion of heart, and by a removal of the causes of war, which are injustice, selfishness, envy, and indifference to the sufferings of others.

The words of Buddha Sâkya-muni are famous:

Hatred never ceases by hatred;
Hatred ceases by love.
This is an unchanging law (Dhammapada 5*).*

Our Lord himself teaches us not to seek revenge, not to take an eye for an eye or a tooth for a tooth, but to be ready to bear injury (cf. Mt 5:38–42). As noted previously, St. Paul says to the Romans: "Never try to get revenge; leave that, my friends, to God's anger . . . If your enemy is hungry, you should give him food, and if he is thirsty, let him drink. Thus you heap red-hot coals on his head. Resist evil and conquer it with good" (Rom 12:19–21).

Violence and war are harsh realities of human existence, brother rises against brother and nation against nation. Some children have not known peace in their lifetime. Some nations or minority groups are cheated of their rights or are simply robbed of them by mightier groups. There are areas of the world where food, medicine, and clothes may be lacking, but where arms are never in short supply.

The arms trade is one of the shameful aspects of some modern societies. Whole peoples are crying out for conflict resolution and for peace and security. Can the religions be silent?

INCULCATE THE VIRTUES
NEEDED FOR PEACE

The preceding reflections have already listed some of the virtues required for peace that the religions are in a good position to inculcate. A few more virtues and values need now be stressed.

Justice is a necessary foundation for peace. If people are deprived of their rights, if they are oppressed and repressed, if they are not allowed to have a voice to claim what is due to them, then the foundations for peace are shaky indeed.

Against the challenge of spiritual poverty shown in isolationism, indifference, and lack of moral sensitivity, religions can reply by insisting that interdependence among people and among countries should not just be tolerated, but should be accepted, loved, and lived. Then it becomes the great moral virtue of solidarity. By solidarity we accept one another as brothers and sisters who are companions in the pilgrimage of life. We are not absolute singles. We are not rivals. We are not threats to one another. We need one another in order to grow and to reach the height of our potential. Each religion can help to nourish this spirit through

[62]

reflection on its religious books, meditation, and prayer. In this way, human conscience and moral sensitivity can be educated and brought to higher levels of performance.

LOVE OF OTHERS

Love of people of other religions is not to be regarded as a mere pious recommendation. It is a real necessity for peace. All religions can cooperate in promoting this. In the concrete, initiatives can take such forms as inculcating esteem for others, willingness to listen and to try to understand, repentance, forgiveness, and reconciliation as earlier explained, and readiness to admire and praise the good, the true and the beautiful in other believers. It should be possible for every believer to find in his or her religious tradition teachings and directives that guide and motivate harmonious relationships with other people, and consequently collaboration with them in the promotion of peace.

INFORM ON THE TERRIBLE EFFECTS OF WAR

Religions can help motivate peace promotion by providing information on the negative and terrible effects of war. After all, war is a proof of human failure, because a more acceptable solution should have been sought to conflicts and disagreements.

Modern warfare in particular involves the use of

weapons with tremendous destructive power, with a consequent heavy toll in human life, among combatants and otherwise, as well as destruction of property and of the structures that human civilization has built up. War brings about the tragedy of refugees; it has a negative effect on the economic, social, and moral lives of millions of people and it is often accompanied by ecological disaster. Pope John Paul II has rightly called war "an adventure without return" (*Speech to Diplomatic Corps accredited to the Holy See*, Jan. 1991). War is a useless massacre that does not generally resolve the problems it professedly set out to solve. It is more human to seek other solutions than the logic of arms. Religions have a duty to conscientize. Religious leaders who take the easier road of simply supporting the political and military position of the leaders of their country who are prosecuting a war, without an effort to help people discern and seek other solutions, may be failing in their responsibilities.

RELIGIONS FOR HEALING

In approaching questions of war and peace, the religions need to bring along the balm of healing. There are wounds that people, individuals and nations, have inflicted on one another physically, morally, and psychologically. Confusion, anxiety, and fear reside in many hearts. Some are tormented by rancor and desire for vendetta for real or merely perceived wrongs. Religions should come to the aid of people in need of healing.

For Christians, Jesus Christ is the visible manifestation of God's love for every human being and of his active desire to heal all human wounds. The greatest of such wounds is sin. And sin is primarily an offense against God. It is often also an offense against one's neighbor. Jesus Christ, through his life, suffering, death, and resurrection, has redeemed humanity from the wound of sin and brought it healing. He has entrusted to his Church the dispensation of his mystery and his Gospel of healing and salvation.

Other religions can articulate how they understand the role of religion in bringing healing. But there is no doubt that, considering the historical nature of humanity as a fallen race (Christians refer here to original sin), the road to peace in human societies will often have to pass through healing.

PEOPLE OF HOPE

In the effort to promote and preserve peace, hope is a virtue for which there is an absolute necessity. Without it, the followers of the various religions can become discouraged. They are painfully aware of their human limitations—they are limited in their understanding, limited in their vision, and limited in their energy and human resources. At times they may even find themselves wondering if they have not taken on too much, if it is really within their power to bring healing and peace to the world.

But it is here that believers should find a spiritual resource in their respective religious commitments that motivates them to act. That resource is hope. Most religions teach their followers to work hard, not to remain passive, and to confront difficult issues. But they further teach that believers are not alone in this struggle.

There is a Power beyond us, whom Christians call God, who supports, fortifies, and indeed makes possible human endeavors for healing and peace. People can work in confidence because they do not rely primarily on their own finite gifts and limited efforts. They have access to divine help, to that added strength without which human beings can neither begin, nor continue, nor bring these projects to a happy conclusion. Peace, at least for Christians, is a gift that is requested of God in prayer.

With convictions such as these, believers will find that they can be united, not only by their commitment to help heal the world and promote peace, but also by their openness to find the vision and the stamina to face the challenges on the way to peace. They are people of hope.

Religions Promoting Practical Initiatives for Peace

In the preceding chapter we have considered how the various religions can help educate people in attitudes that lead to peace or that ensure its preservation. But religions should not limit themselves to conscientization. They should also undertake practical initiatives for peace, individually or jointly. Here are some of the ways in which they can do this.

CORRECT INFORMATION ON OTHER RELIGIONS

Since peace is greatly promoted by good and harmonious interreligious relations, one of the practical ways in which religions can help to build up peace is through nourishing happy relations among themselves. For this, one of the primary requirements is correct information on other religions.

To be sure, goodwill is needed among the followers of the various religions. But this is not enough. If caricatures and incorrect ideas on the other religions exist, practical steps should be taken to right the situation. A planned study of the other religion is needed if relationships are not to stagnate at the superficial level of generalizations and clichés. People who are in positions of leadership or responsibility in each religion have a greater obligation than their coreligionists to undertake a deeper study of the other religion.

Here are two examples of concrete action taken. The Commission for Relations with Muslims established by the Regional Catholic Bishops' Conference of nine French-speaking countries in West Africa produced in 1985 a book that presents Islam to Christians, *Connais-tu ton Frère?*, and in 1989 a book that presents Christianity to Muslims, *Frères dans la Foi au Dieu unique*. In 1990 in France, Catholics collaborated with Muslims and Jews to produce a booklet that presents Judaism, Christianity and Islam to French children (cf. Fr. Bernard-Marie, *La Foi à Trois Voix*, Paris, 1991).

People of one religion can also become better informed on another religion by open-minded conversation with friends of that other religion, especially on the occasion of some celebration marking an event, like the birth of a child, a marriage, a religious initiation or profession, or the death of a member of the community.

Specialized study in the domains of history, sociology,

theology, and other religious sciences also have their place. Here, the universities and similar higher institutes of learning can help, whether they are secular institutions or are affiliated to a particular religion. A university is a center of thought, research, and learning. It is a marketplace where different currents of ideas meet in unfettered communication. Academicians are known for the love and pursuit of knowledge.

It is expected of a university to be objective and thorough in its investigation of the various religions and in imparting the results of these studies. Complex situations of tension or conflict where political, economic, racial, cultural, or religious considerations come into play should be carefully analyzed by higher centers of learning. Thus the public can be objectively and correctly informed.

Light is necessary if darkness is to be chased away. Correct information is needed if centuries-old religious prejudices are to be overcome or reduced. Universities should stubbornly keep informing correctly those bigots who seem to work on the unwritten slogan: "Don't confuse me with facts."

Universities are ideal places for students and lecturers to meet in intellectual discourse on the various religions and provide opportunities for the disentanglement of unhealed historical memories. It is true that mere information is not enough for good interreligious relations. But truth and objective historical information are ingredients to healthy and lasting collaboration.

Here are some examples of activities by universities. The Pontifical Gregorian University in Rome is in academic dialogue with the University of Ankara in Turkey. Exchanges of professors have been arranged. Symposia have been organized allowing the joint participation of Catholic and Muslim lecturers. The Pontifical Institute for Arabic and Islamic Studies, also in Rome, jointly with the Gregorian University, has entered into an academic association with the University of Zaitouna in Tunis. The Institute of Al-Azhar in Cairo has a yearly liaison committee meeting with the Pontifical Council for Interreligious Dialogue and is establishing contacts with the Pontifical University of St. Thomas in Rome. The Center for Muslim-Christian Understanding in Georgetown University in Washington, D.C., has done work to promote correct information on Islam and Christianity.

Since truth is a necessary road to peace, there is no doubt that correct information on other religions is one of the stones needed for a strong foundation for the building that is peace.

Make Goodwill Gestures

Actions speak louder than words. Gestures deliver lessons that register deeper impressions on people than learned discourses.

Religions can therefore build peace by making goodwill gestures to one another. Gestures such as smiles, handshakes, or the equivalent, meeting at the level of daily life, mutual visits on occasions of great significance, mutual listening, and simply the fact of people of many religions sitting together to address a common project or challenge: All these are eloquent signals of friendship and dialogue to the followers in these religions. When such gestures come from the heart, the participants are building peace. Here are some examples.

The Japanese Buddhist family of Rissho Kosei-kai has established friendship with the Catholic Focolare Movement (see page 104) based in Rocca di Papa near Rome. The two movements meet regularly.

In January 1997 the Buddhist University of Mahayulasachu and the nearby monastery in Chiang Mai, in Thailand, invited the leader of the Focolare Movement to address their students, monks, and nuns. From that time, friendship has grown between them and occasional visits have helped to promote mutual understanding.

Imam Warith Deen Mohammed, leader of a group of African American Muslims about two million strong, has friendship links with representatives of the Catholic Church in the United States and with the Focolare Movement. On May 18, 1997, Miss Chiara Lubich of the Focolare Movement was given a grand reception in the Malcolm Shabazz Mosque in Harlem, New York, and in November 2000 the Muslims and the Focolarini held a four-day convention in Washington, D.C.

The Community of Sant'Egidio has good contacts

with people of many religions and this facilitates an annual meeting for peace, as will be explained later.

By far among the most powerful gestures of interreligious peace in our times have been the very warm welcome given to Pope John Paul II on February 24, 2000, by the Sheikh Al-Azhar and the major authorities of that one-thousand-year-old Islamic institution in Cairo and the many meetings between the Pope and Jews, Christians, and Muslims in the Holy Land in March 2000. The modern media, especially television, did excellent service in making these eloquent signals instantly available to people worldwide.

FACE COMMON
PROBLEMS TOGETHER

There are many human problems and challenges that do not respect frontiers of religion or race, and sometimes even of country. Examples are war, hunger, the refugee problem, unemployment, and drugs. If the followers of the various religions strive to face such challenges together, they will be building peace. Later in this book I shall list some interreligious initiatives for peace. Here I wish to mention two initiatives taken at the time of the Gulf War in 1991, especially regarding war, refugees, and migrants.

From March 4 to 6, 1991, Pope John Paul II held a meeting in the Vatican City with seven Patriarchs of the Eastern Churches in the Middle East and Presidents of the Bishops' Conferences of countries more directly involved in the Gulf War. The aim was to study fitting initiatives that would allow the Catholic Church and her institutions to offer a concrete contribution to peace in the Middle East, to promote interreligious collaboration and solidarity, and to help people suffering as a result of the war. A letter of gratitude and support was sent to the Pope on that occasion by Dr. Hamid Algabid, Secretary-General of the Organization of the Islamic Conference. This is a good sign. Moreover, both in setting up an ad hoc committee to help victims of the war, and in his April 1991 Ramadan Message to the World Muslim community, the Pope expressed the desire of the Catholic Church to work together with Muslims to aid the war victims and build structures of a lasting peace. The response has been positive and encouraging.

A second recent example of interreligious collaboration is given by a meeting held in Malta, from April 22 to 24, the same year. The aim was to establish practical cooperation on the global humanitarian problem of refugees and migrants. The meeting was an initiative of three Christian organizations (the International Catholic Migration Commission, the Lutheran World Federation, and the World Council of Churches) and three Muslim organizations (the World Islamic Call Society, the World Muslim Congress, and the World Islamic Call Foundation). It is the first International Christian-Muslim encounter of its kind. Among its declarations, we read: "We affirm that we must work together to ensure that the rights and dignity of all peoples on the move, and their families if separated, are respected and upheld no matter who these people are or wherever they may be found."

These examples of interreligious joining of hands in facing common challenges are steps in the right direction. They are elements of a solid foundation in the education for peace.

Let us now apply this general principle of interreligious collaboration for peace to some concrete areas of life.

DEVELOP JOINT PROJECTS

It is a positive step for peace when people of differing religions undertake joint projects. The more people work together, the better they will accept one another.

I have seen Christians and Muslims join hands to run a leprosy control clinic. There is a country where women of two different religions together approach street women to offer them some means of earning their livelihood worthy of the human person. Buddhists have joined Christians in social service to deprived areas. Rescue of those who are addicted to drugs or assistance to refugees and displaced people are other services that communities of two or more religions can learn to provide together. The more of such practical working together there is in societies, the less difficult will be the promotion of social cohesion and harmony.

If we want peace, we must defend life. Human life comes from God. It is sacred. Almost all religions agree on this. Human life should be protected and respected. Religions will lay a necessary foundation for peace if they teach that human life should be respected in every moment of its existence, from conception right up to natural death. Killing of innocent people is wrong, whether it take the form of abortion, or infanticide, or suicide, or terrorism, or assassination, or euthanasia. To this sad list should be added irresponsible practices of genetic engineering, such as the cloning and use of human embryos for research. The one who despises one life, despises all lives. Religions should educate their followers not to allow any halfway measure in this fundamental question of to be or not to be.

Pope John Paul II in his *Message for World Day of Peace*, 2001, extols the value of human life. "Human life," he says, "cannot be seen as an object to do with as we please, but as the most sacred and inviolable earthly reality. There can be no peace when this most basic good is not protected. It is not possible to invoke peace and despise life" (*Message*, n. 19).

DEFEND THE RIGHTS OF THE CHILD

Religions should find ways to cooperate to teach people to acknowledge and respect the rights of the child. Among other rights, the child has the right to be born, to be loved and cared for by the parents, to be given good education, including religious education, and to be well prepared to start life as an adult.

In the many wars which are sadly not lacking in the world, many children are killed or wounded. Violence is done to them in many other ways. Some boys and girls are forced to serve in the army. Their future is thus compromised and damaged. As Pope John Paul II said in his 1996 *World Day of Peace Message* (n. 2), "The deliberate killing of a child is one of the most disturbing signs of the breakdown of all respect for human life."

We should also not forget those children who suffer because of abuse in their families, poverty, compulsion to work at a tender age and under very harsh conditions, and even the degradation of being sold in order to be used for begging, for drug peddling, or for prostitution.

Some of the violations of the rights of children are sins crying to heaven for vengeance. Religions should not act as if they did not know that all this is happening.

EDUCATION OF YOUTH

The highways to peace are no monopoly of specialists. They are open to all, and especially to young people. Indeed, as Pope John Paul II said in his 1985 *World Peace Day Message*, peace and youth go forward together.

The decisions that the young people of the world make about themselves and their vocation in society will determine to a great extent the prospects for peace today and tomorrow.

Peace and youth also fall together. When war breaks out, it is above all young people who suffer and die. Military cemeteries are a grim reminder of this fact.

Religions should therefore educate youth to form their consciences in favor of peace, to open themselves to dialogue and peaceful negotiation, and to insist with public authorities that national options be in favor of peace.

PROMOTE THE FAMILY

Whatever religions can do together to safeguard, defend, and promote the family is a step toward stability and peace. The family is fundamental in the birth and education of the individual. It is the family that initially equips the child to launch out into the larger society. No religion can afford to ignore this basic cell of society.

If our families are spiritually and morally bankrupt, if they are damaged by tension, quarrels, and refusal to reconcile, if they are distorted by adultery and lack of love, if they are scattered by divorce, litigation, and separation, then the rest of society is in deep trouble. The crisis of society in a way begins from crisis in the family.

Religion should manifest itself in works of justice, respect for human rights and dignity, development and human promotion in the full sense of the concept. The road to peace passes necessarily that way. Religion would evaporate into arid philosophy if it did not grapple with situations of hunger, inadequate housing, disease, illiteracy, and unemployment. Similar remarks apply to discrimination against people because of their race, religion, social class, sex, or place of origin.

The challenge of poverty needs special mention. There are individuals and whole peoples who do not have the minimum requirement of food, water, health care, education, housing, or employment for dignified human existence. They can sometimes be partly responsible for their fate. But more often their poverty is largely due to the short-sighted policies of their rulers, the dishonesty or corruption of people in public life, or the economic decisions of the richer countries, which either ignore or even exploit the weaknesses of the so-called Third World countries.

To promote overall human development is to prepare for peace. Excessive inequalities among peoples in the economic, social, and cultural fields arouse tensions and are a threat to peace. Peace and prosperity are goods that belong to the whole human race. They cannot be enjoyed, and are not meant to be enjoyed, in a selfish way and at the cost of other peoples (cf. Paul VI, *Populorum Progressio*, 76–77; John Paul II, *Centesimus Annus*, 27). When, therefore, the various religions join hands to uplift the poor and the disinherited, and to help them help themselves, they are working for peace.

The homeless, the unemployed, the sick, and those groaning under the burden of grinding poverty, crushing underdevelopment, or ever heavier external debts—these people are crying for attention if we are to install genuine peace. Poverty not addressed can lead to dehumanization and despair. And a hungry person can easily become an angry person and a ready tool in the hands of a violent revolutionary.

It is to be noted that in societies where people are suffering under such unjust situations, religious extremists can cash in. They may find it easy to arouse the support of the suffering poor, who are the vast majority, by making extravagant religious claims. The temptation that the answer to such situations of suffering is a return to what is presented as an original or pure form of a certain religion is an easy one. Violent reactions can easily be provoked.

The effective and permanent response is not a crackdown on religious fanatics, even though some restraint on their activities is unavoidable. The real answer is joint action by people of all the religions in the area, together with other citizens, to promote justice, development, sound economic programs, honesty in private and public life, and willingness on the part of the rich to show serious solidarity with the poor. Peace stands on the pillars of love, truth, freedom, development, justice, and solidarity.

JOINT CONCERN OVER THE USE OF THE EARTH'S RESOURCES

Concern with the endangered earth, and therefore with ecological harmony, should not be regarded as something neutral by the world religions. "The dominion granted to man by the Creator," says Pope John Paul II, "is not an absolute power . . . A true concept of development cannot ignore the use of the elements of nature, the renewability of resources and the consequences of haphazard industrialization—three considerations which alert our consciences to the moral dimensions of development" (*Sollicitudo Rei Socialis*, 34). After all, we are not absolute masters of created goods, but administrators who must be attentive to the consequences of our use of them to present and future generations.

The experts tell us that 20 percent of humanity consumes 80 percent of the earth's resources, leaving only 20 percent to four-fifths of humanity. Moreover, certain rich countries restrain food production for the sake of balancing market prices, while there are poor countries whose inhabitants do not have enough to eat. And no one needs the experts to know that the earth's resources can be devastated or slowly depleted by greed, carelessness, and war.

Here is a rich area for people of many religions to co-operate for peace building.

DISARMAMENT AND ARMS TRADE

Many states spend huge sums of money in building large armies and equipping them with ever more destructive and expensive armaments. The religions cannot remain unconcerned.

There are poor countries in the world where food, medicine, and clothing may be lacking, but where arms are never in short supply. The arms trade is one of the shameful aspects of some modern societies. Whole peoples are groaning under intense suffering and are crying out for liberation, right order of priorities, disarmament, and peace. Can the religions turn a deaf ear to these groanings?

PROMOTE RECONCILIATION

The promotion of reconciliation between people is another necessary road to peace, as has earlier been underlined. And here religions are particularly well qualified to help, because they can make appeals to many needed spiritual considerations.

Depending on local situations, reconciliation is sometimes needed between people of differing ethnic or linguistic origins, or of social status, or of economic standing. Between the oppressed and their oppressors, truth, justice, repentance, readiness for reparation, and reconciliation are needed. Religions are well placed to inculcate the virtues of self-control, justice, and love toward others, and acknowledgment of fault where one has done wrong. The wise Buddha tells us: "Between the person who wins in battle one thousand times and thereby has one thousand enemies, and the one who wins only over self, this latter is the best of the winners of every battle" (*Dhammapada* 103, in *Canone Buddista*, Torino 1968, p. 112). The Lord Jesus Christ gives us the master commandment of love: "You shall love your neighbor as yourself" (Mt 22:39).

Reconciliation is particularly difficult after a war. Those who prosecute war generally tell us that they want thereby to "solve" problems. But they leave in their wake victims and relics of destruction that do not facilitate reconciliation, unless, of course, they were seeking the silent and cold peace of the cemetery.

All people of goodwill, and in particular the followers of world religions, are called to rise above the culture of war in order to install a culture of peace. Where a human problem really exists, there must be a peaceful and honorable way to solve it. War is not inevitable. The arms industry, and the arms trafficking that almost inevitably ensues, should give way to investments in agriculture and industry, thus building up the economy for the benefit of all. Swords should be hammered into plowshares and spears into sickles (cf. Is 2:4).

If the religions do not promote reconciliation, who will do it?

The Burden of History: Healing of Historical Memories

Reconciliation is no easy virtue when historical memories weigh down a people. The heavy burden of oppression, violence, conflict, or war which brought about much suffering among one's forebears cannot be easily laid aside. It leaves a residue of fear, suspicion, division, and sometimes even hatred among families, ethnic groups, or whole peoples. Human logic sometimes yields to the temptation to revenge, to make the offenders or their children pay dearly for their deeds, or to teach them a lesson that they will never forget.

These are harsh realities that put the goodwill of promoters of reconciliation to a hard test. One solution is to facilitate a correct reading of history. The history of conflict with other peoples should be written and read without bias. This is not an easy recommendation. It demands the effort to try to understand why the other people feel the way they do. History is often written by the victors or the dominant group. To be truly objective it needs to take into account the perceptions of all the parties involved. Rarely are mistakes all on one side. National historical accounts should therefore be on the watch for the tendency to become slanted in favor of one's country, ethnic group, or religion.

Respect for differences is another useful recommendation for genuine relationships. To deny differences is to deny the identity of the other. And even when the suppression of differences appears to be successful, it is often a case of only an apparent peace, because a volatile situation is created that is generally a prelude to fresh outbreaks of disagreement, tension, or violence. Historical records that are unpleasant have to be dealt with honestly and with moral courage.

No matter how difficult the effort at the healing of historical memories may be, religions owe it to humanity to engage in this together in order to build a just and lasting peace. To accept the past is a condition for realistically facing the future. Sincerity and truth are needed. Past wrongs should be acknowledged and regretted. Pardon should be sought and given. Only then will true reconciliation be firmly established.

LEARNING TO EXERCISE
SELF-CRITICISM AND ASK PARDON

The difficult exercise of self-criticism and asking for pardon has to be learned by the various religions. The more they practice this singly and together, the better they will pave the way to peace.

Acceptance of fault where it exists, willingness to engage in self-criticism, asking and giving pardon, and willingness to seek reconciliation are virtues badly needed for true and lasting peace. The ability to repent and ask for forgiveness is not a sign of weakness but rather of moral strength. An individual should not presume that he or she is never wrong. And a religion should not start from the premise that all its followers have always lived up to the highest demands of its ideals.

Pope John Paul II led the Catholic Church in a ceremony in St. Peter's Basilica, Vatican City, on March 12, 2000, to show how believers can engage in an examination of conscience and ask pardon of God and also of their fellow human beings. He had earlier, in 1994, explained the meaning of the ceremony. The Church, in his words, "should become more fully conscious of the sinfulness of her children, recalling all those times in history when they departed from the spirit of Christ and his Gospel and, instead of offering to the world the witness of a life inspired by the values of faith, indulged in ways of thinking and acting which were truly forms of counter-witness and scandal. Although she is holy because of her incorporation into Christ, the Church does not tire of doing penance: before God and man she always acknowledges as her own her sinful sons and daughters" (*Tertio Millennio Adveniente*, 33).

Jesus Christ forgave those who were crucifying him. He prayed for them: "Father, forgive them; they do not know what they are doing" (Lk 23:34). Religions should teach people to do the same, to forgive and to promote reconciliation (cf. Pope John Paul II, *Message for World Day of Peace*, 2001, n. 21). If all religious families engaged in a similar exercise, an important purification of hearts, humble approach to history and to other people, and greater awareness of human solidarity would help lead the world to greater harmony and peace.

In this chapter we have considered some of the practical ways in which the religions can advance the cause of peace, singly and together. But there is one more activity that needs a whole chapter to itself because of its key importance. It is prayer for peace. That will now engage our attention.

Religions and Prayer for Peace

Religion of its very nature has to do with what is most profound in a human being. We talk of the spirit, the heart, the mind, the interior of the person. Religion refers primarily to relations between the human being and God the Creator, and secondarily to relations with other people and with creation. Prayer is a major dimension of religion.

In the contribution of the religions of the world to peace, the prayer aspect could not be missing. Considering, however, the great variety among the existing religions in the world, one has to proceed carefully in the examination of this matter.

Every religion has its concept and tradition of prayer. In general, there is reference to the human being seeking or having contact with God the Creator, or the Supreme Being, or at least a superior being. Buddhists, because of the nature of their tradition, speak of meditation rather than of prayer.

I think it is best if I as a Christian explain briefly what prayer means to a Christian. The reader who is of another religious persuasion is requested to spell out the understanding of prayer in that tradition. Thereafter, our examination of the contribution of the religions to peace through prayer will move on with greater fruitfulness.

For a Christian, prayer is the raising of one's mind and heart to God. The praying soul, out of the depths of a humble and contrite heart, seeks to appear in God's presence, begging for the gift of contact with God. "For me," says St. Thérèse of Lisieux, "prayer is a surge of the heart; it is a simple look turned toward heaven; it is a cry of recognition and love, embracing both trial and joy" (*Manuscrits Autobiographiques*, C 25r).

Prayer can be expressed in words, or gestures, or aspirations, or just elevations of the soul without being articulated in words. As one of the highest acts of a human being, prayer comes from the soul, or the spirit, or, as graphically put, from the heart. Those whose hearts are far from God do not offer the best of prayers. God knows our heart even before we pray; yet it is useful for us to open our heart to God. The heart is the place of desires, of decision, of truth, of encounter with God. It is in the heart that a person chooses life or death, chooses to say yes to God and obey his commandments, or to forsake God, the fountain of living water and to dig to oneself leaky cisterns that can hold no water. It is in the heart that a person chooses to love the neighbor and seek reconciliation and peace, or to do otherwise (cf. Jer 2:13; *Catechism of the Catholic Church*, 2563).

Christian prayer is moreover understood as communion with God, as a covenant relationship of man with God who is Father, Son, and Holy Spirit. God takes the initiative. The Holy Spirit guides us how to pray. Christian prayer is generally offered to God the Father, through Jesus Christ his Son, in the unity of the Holy Spirit, although one can also pray to Christ or to the Holy Spirit.

The intentions encompassed by prayer are as wide as the acts of the virtue of religion, namely, adoration, praise, thanksgiving, propitiation for our offenses and petitions. For a Christian, the model prayer is the "Our Father," taught by Jesus Christ himself and including seven invocations which contain all that we can ask of God.

There are many forms of Christian prayer: liturgical prayer, that is, official prayer in the name of the Church (made up of the sacraments, other public rites, and the Divine Office), then devotional prayers of individuals or communities, meditative prayer, contemplation, silent adoration, and intercessory prayer.

As indicated earlier, people of other religions may now articulate to themselves what their tradition teaches them regarding prayer. This will make the following reflections more meaningful.

PRECIOUS CONTRIBUTIONS
FROM PRAYER

Some religious traditions speak of meditation along with prayer. For them, meditation refers rather to calm reflection on major truths of religion, on events touching human life on earth, on the purpose of human existence, on questions of moral good and evil, on God the Creator who alone explains all created reality, and on man's earthly pilgrimage, its direction, and its conclusion. For such religions, meditation is an important preparation for prayer and a proximate introduction to it.

In prayer the human soul makes a great effort at sincerity, honesty, truth, humility, and acceptance of personal responsibility. In the vertical dimension of relations with God, the soul at prayer acknowledges God as the Creator, as the one whose will people should follow if there is to be tranquillity in society, and as the one who is offended by sins of all kinds. By prayer—intense, humble, confident, and persevering—the soul opens itself to the saving action of God. Meditation and prayer help believers to reflect, to see themselves as they are and not just as they would like to be seen. A consequence is that the of-fender is rendered more willing to acknowledge faults, to repent, and to ask for forgiveness, instead of engaging in pointless self-justification. This attitude is helpful toward peace.

In the horizontal dimension of relationship with other human beings, meditation and prayer help us acknowledge the rights of others, to realize that we have duties toward them, and to accept if there have been lapses in our ac-tions. Mutual esteem and acceptance of other people with all their differences, and finally love of others, are what we can hope for from sincere meditation and prayer. They are highly conducive to peace.

Meditation and prayer should also help to dispose people to a proper attitude toward the goods of the earth that God has created for the use of all.

Peace a Gift to Be Obtained by Prayer

From what has just been said, it follows that an important role of religions in educating for peace is to teach their fol-lowers the necessity of prayer for peace. We should not forget that before being a product of human activity, peace is first of all a gift that we must request of God. When Pope John Paul II invited representatives of various world religions to pray for peace at Assisi in 1986, the International Year for Peace, one newspaper came out with an editorial entitled: "It is not enough to pray for peace, it is necessary to work for it." But what the Pope wanted to stress was the opposite dimension: "It is not enough to work for peace, it is necessary to pray"! Prayer makes us realize both our weakness and our strength: our weakness, because we are fragile creatures limited in our understanding and sinful; our strength, because we are not alone; we are helped by the Creator, who will not abandon us. Thus prayer creates the conditions of humility and hope that can sustain action for peace.

The Pope, of course, does appreciate the importance of governments and international relations in the promotion of peace. But his intention in calling the World Day of Prayer for Peace at Assisi was to underline the importance of prayer. In his opening address to the interreligious assembly, he said: "The coming together of so many religious leaders to pray is in itself an invitation today to the world to become aware that there exists another dimension of peace and another way of promoting it which is not a result of negotiations, political compromises, or economic bargainings. It is the result of prayer, which, in the diversity of religions, expresses a relationship with a supreme power that surpasses our human capacities alone" (*Opening Address* in Pont. Commission "Justitia et Pax," *Assisi: World Day of Prayer for Peace*, p. 87).

Jesus Christ himself, the "Prince of Peace" (Eph 2:14),

made clear to his disciples that peace is God's gift: "Peace I bequeath to you, my own peace I give you, a peace the world cannot give, this is my gift to you" (Jn 14:27).

DISPOSITIONS FOR PEACE
NOURISHED BY PRAYER

Gathering together the contributions to peace that prayer can make, we can list them as follows:

Prayer helps open up the human heart to God the Most High and to his commandments, his ways, his laws written in the human heart or conscience.

Prayer helps people open out to their neighbors, to establish due contacts with them in relationships of respect, understanding, esteem, and love. Hence Pope John Paul II says in his *Message for World Day of Peace*, 1992: "Prayer is the bond which most effectively unites us: it is through prayer that believers meet one another at a level where inequalities, misunderstandings, bitterness, and hostility are overcome, namely before God, the Lord and Father of all. Prayer, as the authentic expression of a right relationship with God and with others, is already a positive contribution to peace" (*Message*, 4).

A prayerful attitude teaches people the relative value of the things of this world. Most religions inculcate some degree of detachment from earthly goods, some form of asceticism or spiritual self-control. This is useful for peace building when we recall that many conflicts are due to people's greed, uncontrolled desire for earthly goods, and unwillingness to share them with others.

The road to peace is slow and sometimes rough. It demands patience, perseverance, humility, and a willingness to start all over again. Meditation and prayer are highly conducive to these virtues.

Is it any wonder that many believers appreciate that for peace they have to pray?

BELIEVERS COME
TOGETHER TO PRAY

For all the above-mentioned reasons, believers in the various religions see the need not only to pray as individuals and in their respective religious communities, but also on some special occasions to come together to pray for peace.

The most impressive occasion when believers in many religions gathered to pray for peace was on the World Day of Prayer for peace at Assisi on October 27, 1986, at the invitation of Pope John Paul II. Explaining the significance of the event in his Christmas Address to the Cardinals and other workers of the Roman Curia two months afterward, the Pope said: "At Assisi, in an extraordinary way, there was the discovery of the unique value that prayer has for peace; indeed it was seen that it is impossible to have peace without prayer, the prayer of all, each one in his own identity and in search of the truth . . . We can indeed maintain that every authentic prayer is called forth by the Holy Spirit, who is mysteriously present in the heart of every person" (Address on Dec. 22, 1986, in Pont. Commission Justice and Peace, *Assisi World Day of Prayer for Peace*, Rome, 1986, p. 146).

In January 1993, the Pope again invited Christians, Jews, and Muslims in Europe to come to Assisi to pray for peace in Europe, and especially in the Balkans.

In 1999, in the context of a four-day meeting of two hundred representatives of twenty world religions in Vatican City, there was organized a two-hour period of prayer by each religion in a separate place.

The religions in Japan—Buddhists, Shintoists, Catholics, and Protestants—taking a cue from the Assisi event of 1986, organized on Mount Hiei, Kyoto, in 1987 a meeting of world religions to pray for peace. A yearly commemoration has been done since then, around the anniversary of the atomic bombing of Hiroshima and Nagasaki.

The Community of Saint Egidio, a Catholic lay association centered in Rome, has organized a yearly gathering of people of many religions to reflect on peace and pray. More will be said on this later.

There are many local groups around the world that are convinced that it is not enough to discuss peace, but that we should also pray for it. Their prayers take many forms. Indeed the desire of people of different religions to pray together is increasing and has made it necessary for us now to say a word on interreligious prayer.

The desire of people who believe in God to pray should be praised and encouraged. It is right and fitting that we creatures acknowledge our dependence on God on our knees in humble prayer. Peace, as was said above, is first and foremost a gift we request from God, before being a fruit of human efforts.

The desire to pray together is also good. We human beings are social by nature. None of us is an island.

It is to be appreciated, however, that prayer and faith are closely related. Faith is manifested in prayer. And prayer builds up faith and articulates it.

To the extent that people believe the same thing, they can share the same prayer. The most normal form of prayer, therefore, is that which has grown up in a particular faith community and which is therefore distinctive. Thus we can talk of a Jewish prayer, a Muslim prayer, a Christian prayer, even of a Catholic prayer.

All Christians believe in one God in three Persons: Father, Son, and Holy Spirit; and in Jesus Christ, the Son of God, God and Man and Savior of all humanity. Christian prayer therefore has a trinitarian character: It is generally addressed, as has been said already, to the Father, through Jesus Christ his Son, in the unity of the Holy Spirit. Catholics, Orthodox, Anglicans, Presbyterians, Lutherans, Baptists, and other Christians each have their own specific prayers and worship rites. On special occasions they can have ecumenical prayer. If such a prayer takes a formal or official form, there will be need for the approval of their leaders. This generally raises little problem when the texts are carefully prepared by competent people.

The theological problems become greater when Christians, Muslims, Hindus, and people of Traditional Religions want to say the same prayer together. There is generally not much of a problem if at a social function, like a town meeting, a meal, or a fund-raising event, the chairman asks a person of one religion to say an opening or closing prayer. If the person frames a general prayer which all the people present can sincerely offer, they will have little difficulty in answering "Amen."

The greater problem arises with formal interreligious prayers arranged on national days, times of war, thanksgiving celebrations, or solemn public prayers for peace. Even presuming that the participants all hold to strict monotheism and pray to the same God, there still remain the problems of the content of the prayer and especially of the real danger of scandal that would be caused by the appearance or danger of relativism and syncretism, whether real or merely apparent. Relativism is the theological error that one religion is as good as another. Syncretism is the error of taking elements from the various religions in order to construct and serve up something new. For these reasons, interreligious prayer in this form of looking for common formulas is not advisable.

There is the other possibility of multireligious prayer. It can take the form of people of one religion praying on their own while others stand by in reverence. Then those of another religion perform their own prayer. Although less objectionable than strict interreligious prayer, this has also its difficulties. It is easy for people to misunderstand it and to interpret it wrongly. Care is needed. Religious leaders should not fail in their duty to be watchful and helpful.

In their prayer for peace, it is best and safest if each religious tradition prays in a separate place according to its identity. Nevertheless, the following suggestions may be of help in the continued study of what forms of interreligious prayer for peace would be appropriate: Provision should be made for periods of silent prayer. I have seen it work out beautifully at gatherings of people of many religions. Silence encourages interiority, reflection, and raising of mind and heart to God. It both achieves letting people be fully themselves and, at the same time, their doing it together with others. Some symbols such as the lighting of candles by representatives of the participating religions, exchange of signs of friendship or peace, and some form of expression of joint commitment to harmony may be found helpful.

We must thank God that people are realizing more and more the necessity of prayer for peace.

EIGHT

Some Interreligious Initiatives for Peace

In the preceding pages, thought has generally been concentrated on what the religions can do, or should do, to advance peace. Occasionally what they have actually done has been mentioned. It seems right in this chapter, even at the risk of some repetition, to list some of the more outstanding interreligious initiatives or projects for peace actually undertaken in the past three decades. The list does not pretend to be exhaustive, but hopefully it will be enough to show that religions have not been idle. It can also help encourage further action. As far as possible, chronological order will be followed in listing these initiatives.

The World Conference on Religion and Peace (W.C.R.P.) was established in 1968 by Christians, Buddhists, Muslims, Jews, and Hindus with the aim of promoting collaboration among people of various religions in favor of peace. W.C.R.P. is recognized by the United Nations Organization as a Non-Governmental Organization. It takes initiatives to promote disarmament, to help to remedy underdevelopment, to reconcile warring groups, to defend the oppressed and to promote peace education. It has, for example, undertaken initiatives for peace and reconciliation in Bosnia-Herzegovina, in Kosovo, in Sierra Leone, in Ethiopia and Eritrea, in Liberia, and in the Middle East.

W.C.R.P. has held world assemblies in Kyoto in 1970, Louvain in 1974, Princeton, N.J., in 1979, Nairobi in 1984, Melbourne in 1989, Riva del Garda in 1994, and Amman in 1999. Each world assembly records more participants than the preceding one, including heads of government and religious leaders from such traditions as the Buddhist, Christian, Confucian, Hindu, Jain, Jewish, Muslim, Shinto, Sikh, Traditional Religions, and Zoroastrian.

Besides W.C.R.P. International, which has its office in New York, there are Regional W.C.R.P. Organizations on the continental level. The association also exists at the national level in many countries and that is where it can have deep roots and be more effective in tackling local problems. As an example of what has been done, I can mention one of the actions taken by the Japan Chapter of W.C.R.P. In November 1992 it brought together a group of Arabs (Christians and Muslims) and Jews to reflect on the Middle East conflict. The participants recognized that the Japanese, being neutral, could make a contribution by bringing all the sides together.

W.C.R.P. is a proof, if any were needed, that it is possible for believers in the major religions in the world to come together to do something to promote justice and peace, without necessarily discussing their particular religious beliefs and practices.

THE 1986 ASSISI WORLD DAY OF PRAYER FOR PEACE

On October 27, 1986, Pope John Paul invited representatives of the major world religions to come to Assisi to pray and fast in promotion of peace during the International Year of Peace declared by the United Nations.

The response was enthusiastic. In addition to representatives of the various families of Christianity, there came to Assisi leaders of Jews, Buddhists, Muslims, Hindus, Shintoists, Sikhs, Jainists, Traditional Religions, Baha'i, and Zoroastrians. The Muslims came from such countries as Turkey, Saudi Arabia, India, Bangladesh, Pakistan, Libya, Algeria, Morocco, and the Ivory Coast.

At the Assisi celebration, each religious family prayed

separately according to its own tradition. The celebration attracted the attention of the world to the fact that in order to have peace, we need not only governments, the United Nations, and negotiations, but also prayer, religion, and the help of Almighty God.

The Assisi event has inspired other initiatives, as we shall soon recount. Moreover, in January 1993 there was another event in Assisi, although on a smaller scale. It was during the war in the Balkans. Pope John Paul II, together with the Catholic Bishops of Europe, organized a vigil, a fast, and a Solemn Mass in Assisi with the intention of praying for peace in Europe, especially in the Balkans. Representatives of various Christian denominations and also leaders from the Jewish and Muslim communities in different countries in Europe were invited to this weekend of prayer. The Muslim participation on this occasion was very significant.

RELIGIONS OF JAPAN ORGANIZE PRAYER FOR PEACE

The Buddhists in Japan were preparing to celebrate in 1987 the twelfth centenary of the coming of Buddhism to their country. But their participation in the Assisi World Day of Prayer for peace in 1986 gave them the idea to widen the perspective of the celebrations. Under the leadership of the venerable Etai Yamada, Abbot of the Buddhist Mount Hiei monastery near Kyoto, the religions of Japan (Buddhists, Shintoists, Catholics, and Protestants) invited representatives of the major religions of the world to come to Mount Hiei to pray for peace. The date chosen for the event was at the beginning of August in order to commemorate the atomic bombing of Hiroshima and Nagasaki, which took place on August 6 and 9, 1945. The celebration borrowed many ideas from the 1986 Assisi event and sent a powerful signal that religions are for peace.

Every year the religions of Japan gather to pray for peace in August in those two cities where the horrors of war are all too visible. The tenth-anniversary celebration in 1997 was particularly solemn. As I visited Hiroshima, the phrase that kept coming to my mind was the one inscribed on the commemorative plaque: "No more Hiroshima."

THE COMMUNITY OF ST. EGIDIO

A Catholic lay association based in Rome, the Community of St. Egidio, which was begun by young people in 1968, through the special organization it set up, "People and Religions," has developed a growing collaboration between various believers in favor of peace. Members of the Community of St. Egidio had helped with practical details of the Prayer for Peace event in Assisi in 1986. They then responded to Pope John Paul II's appeal to keep alive "the spirit of Assisi." "People and Religions" has brought distinguished representatives of the world religions, together with heads of state and other leaders from governments or international organizations, to reflect on action for peace. Its yearly rally has been held since 1987 in Rome, Warsaw, Bari, Malta, Brussels, Milan, Assisi, Padua-Venice, Bucharest, and Lisbon.

These conventions are marked by plenary assemblies, small group discussions according to themes or countries involved in some ongoing conflict, prayer by each religion in a separate place, and a concluding session in which a communiqué on peace is read and a sign of peace is exchanged. The fact that each year an even higher number of participants and an impressive body of statesmen do take part is evidence of the support and credibility that these conventions have gathered.

The most spectacular success in peace building by the Community of St. Egidio has been its mediation that led to peace between the government and the guerrillas in Mozambique. But the organization has also been at work to help toward peace in Algeria, in the Democratic Republic of the Congo, in Guatemala and Kosovo. It has also developed useful ecumenical contacts with the Orthodox Churches, for example, in Romania and in Constantinople.

THE FOCOLARE MOVEMENT

The Work of Mary, popularly known as the Focolare Movement, with its headquarters in Rocca di Papa near Rome, is a Catholic lay movement that strives to live the charism of unity and love according to the Gospel. As the movement developed from its small beginnings in 1943, it has in the past two decades promoted many ecumenical and interreligious contacts.

The members of the Focolare Movement also gave practical assistance with the organization of the 1986 Prayer for Peace in Assisi.

In the ecumenical field, the Movement has lively contacts with the Ecumenical Patriarch of Constantinople, with the Archbishop of Canterbury, and with many Lutherans in Germany.

Interreligious contacts have been built up gradually with a Buddhist organization, the Rissho Kosei-Kai, and with African-American Muslims in the United States. Chiara Lubich, the founder of the Focolare Movement, has been invited to speak to gatherings of Buddhists in Japan, in a Buddhist monastery and university in Thailand, and in a mosque in Harlem, New York. More recently she has been invited to address Hindus in Coimbatore and in other places in India.

The Movement has also built up a network of Muslim friends who follow the ideals of this Christian movement while remaining loyal to their own religion. Such a group exists even in wartorn Algeria.

The Focolare Movement operates by living Christian witness and gestures of esteem and love rather than by direct efforts at peace building. But there is no doubt that its contribution is an important stone in the foundation of the cathedral that is peace.

A listing of initiatives for peace promoted by religions, such as I have undertaken, will unavoidably have the defect of being incomplete. May I at least mention, no matter how briefly, a few more positive steps that believers have taken that also in one way or the other help build peace.

The Center for World Thanksgiving in Dallas, Texas, promotes thanksgiving at all levels, but especially among religions and by religions. It succeeded in persuading the United Nations Plenary Assembly on November 20, 1997, to declare the year 2000 the International Year of Thanksgiving. The spirit it engenders helps build peace.

The Inter-Faith Network for the United Kingdom works to build good relations between the communities of all the major religions in Britain: Baha'i, Buddhist, Christian, Hindu, Jain, Jewish, Muslim, Sikh, and Zoroastrian. It has more than eighty member bodies. It aims to make Britain a country marked by mutual understanding and respect among religions. The Network is a sign of hope on the way to harmony and peace.

In August 2000, several people took the initiative of gathering a thousand representatives of most of the religions in the world to meet for four days in New York. The Millennium World Peace Summit of Religious and Spiritual Leaders had the promotion of peace as its priority. Even if one cannot hope to achieve very much in mutual discussion among so many people in a few days, the general signal given to the world that people of various religions want peace was unmistakable.

These and many other initiatives of people of various religions not mentioned, while acknowledging that religious differences may aggravate conflicts, nevertheless demonstrate a conviction that there is hope that many moral values shared across religious frontiers can provide a basis for communities and states to live together in harmony and peace. And these initiatives are practical ways of taking some action to make this harmony and peace a reality.

SAMPLES OF INTERRELIGIOUS HARMONY

Let us close this chapter with a listing of some happy samples of harmony, greater justice, and peace that came about as a result of interreligious action.

~ In the United Kingdom, Muslims join Christians to fight against abortion in the Society for the Protection of Unborn Children.

~ In Bosnia-Herzegovina, Christian, Jewish, and Muslim religious leaders strive to promote reconciliation.

~ In the Philippines, the Silsilah Christian-Muslim Dialogue Movement in Zamboanga has been involved in several projects of education for the poor, building homes for the homeless, protecting the dignity of women, and feeding the hungry. And on the island of Jolo in the same country, Christians and Muslims demonstrated together when a young man was kidnapped and beheaded.

✒ In Pakistan, the National Commission for Christian-Muslim Relations sponsors and helps centers for detoxification and rehabilitation and homes for lepers and does relief work for the poor. In the same country, Christians and Muslims demonstrated together against the inclusion of religion on citizens' identity cards and against the Blasphemy Law, which can easily be abused.

✒ In India, Hindu and Christian members of a dialogue group visited together to calm feelings, which were running high at the time of the destruction of the Ayodya mosque.

✒ In Japan, the Rissho Kosei-kai Buddhist Association encourages its members to omit one meal a week and donate the money for poor countries. It also sends teams of people to work with the refugees in Rwanda.

✒ In Sierra Leone, Christian and Muslim religious leaders have acted as mediators for reconciliation and peace between the government and the R.U.F.

✒ When Ethiopia and Eritrea were unfortunately at war, religious leaders—Orthodox, Catholic, Evangelical, and Muslim—made a joint appeal for peace in September 1998.

During the January-February 1991 Gulf War, there were many cities in Europe and North Africa where Christians and Muslims, and sometimes Jews, met together to pray and to make joint declarations in favor of justice and peace.

No matter how difficult peace building may be, one cannot say that religions are absent from the construction site. With varying degrees of effectiveness and commitment, they have contributed. It seems only right that since I am a Catholic, I should now record some of the actions taken by the Catholic Church to promote peace. This may encourage the reader of another religious family to articulate what his or her community has done on the matter.

The Catholic Church and Peace Promotion

PREACHING THE GOSPEL OF JESUS CHRIST

The most fundamental way in which the Catholic Church promotes peace is by preaching the Gospel of Jesus Christ. This is a Gospel of love of others, of humility, of justice, of reconciliation, and of service. It is a Gospel based on the new commandment of Christ, that of mutual love, after the example of Christ: "As I have loved you, so you also should love one another. This is how all will know that you are my disciples" (Jn 13:34–35).

This Gospel preaches that people will have peace and be blessed if they live the spirit of the eight Beatitudes (cf. Mt 5:9 ff .), if they are ready to forgive and even go the extra mile, and if they will be converted to God in the interiority of their hearts and worship him in spirit and in truth (cf. Mt 5:38–42; Jn 4:24).

Interior peace is Christ's gift to his disciples. It is a peace that the world cannot give (cf. Jn 14:27). Our peace is centered on Christ. "He is our peace," St. Paul tells the Ephesians (Eph 2:14). Christ came to break down the dividing walls of enmity. By his blood, shed for all on the cross, he has established peace for all with God, and also peace between people who are divided. Christ came to bring reconciliation and peace. The prophet Isaiah already called him "Prince of Peace" (Is 9:6).

CONVERSION OF HEART

Conversion of heart is central to the preaching and work of the Church. Peace is not possible if hearts are not converted toward God and neighbor in love. "I shall give you a new heart," the Lord promises us through the prophet Ezekiel (Ezk 36:24). With the prophet Isaiah, the Church in document after document, in appeal after appeal, asks the people who promote the culture of violence and death to knock their swords into plowshares (cf. Is 2:4). Hardened positions and intransigence have now to be exchanged for understanding and flexibility. Years and years of nonacceptance of others, of unwillingness to share the good things of the earth with one's brothers and sisters, and of abuse of religion to justify discrimination or violence, should now, in the light of Christ, be turned into repentance, reconciliation, mutual forgiveness, and love. The Sacrament of Penance is institutionalized reconciliation with God and neighbor.

One of the greatest lessons that Jesus taught us was that while hanging in agony on the cross, he forgave and prayed for those who were crucifying him: "Father, forgive them; they do not know what they are doing" (Lk 23:34). The Church preaches this not-very-easy doctrine. This is a golden road to peace.

BALANCED SOCIAL TEACHING

The Church "which has long experience in human affairs" (Paul VI, *Populorum Progressio*, 13), has evolved a rich body of thought and teaching on many aspects of human life and earthly realities. The Church helps all men and women to reflect on the truth concerning human life on earth, on human dignity, on human rights and obligations, and on the good ordering of society. Hence the Church has a well developed body of doctrine on marriage and the family, on capital and labor, on authority as service, on the universal destination of earthly goods, on relations between rich and poor, whether individuals or states, on interdependence and solidarity among peoples, and on the need to resolve differences by negotiation and discussion rather than by violence and war.

The Church teaches Christians that to discharge their

duties as citizens is a necessary dimension of their religious commitment and condemns the negative action of those Christians who are not good citizens (cf. *Gaudium et Spes*, 43).

Authority is to be understood as service, following Jesus Christ, who came not to be served, but to serve and to give his life as a ransom for all (cf. Mk 10:45). The Church teaches that authority in the final analysis comes from God and that obedience to lawful authorities is part of what it means to be a good Christian (cf. Rm 13:1–7; *Catechism of the Catholic Church* 2234–2240; *Gaudium et Spes*, 43).

All this is highly conducive to peace and harmony.

Integral Human Development

The Catholic Church strives to promote integral human development, the development of the whole person and of every person (Paul VI, *Populorum Progressio*, 14). As Pope Paul VI puts it, the development of peoples is the new name for peace (op. cit., 76). For this reason the Church strives in various ways to promote people's good health, to conduct medical institutions, to defend the rights of children, women, and oppressed peoples, and to take practical initiatives in the educational field. Many religious orders, especially of consecrated women, have been founded precisely to serve the orphan, the poor, the old, and the sick. Monks and nuns and other consecrated people vow to live lives of evangelical simplicity and sharing.

It is clear that if people are undernourished or downright hungry, homeless and unemployed; if they are sick, illiterate, and without social security; if they are oppressed, repressed, and exploited; then there is little hope for peace. Such disinherited people can easily be hijacked by a revolutionary who promises to bring them into the promised land of equality, enjoyment, and contentment through the rough paths of revolution, violence, killing, looting, and combating the rich and against the established order. In short, it is clear that if we want peace, we must promote development. The Catholic Church strives to promote this conviction and to live it in practice.

VATICAN II ON PEACE

The Second Vatican Council, a solemn assembly of 3,068 Bishops of the Catholic Church in four sessions of two or three months each year from 1962 to 1965, gave great importance to peace in its deliberations, especially in its Pastoral Constitution on the Church in the World of Today.

This Constitution says that the Gospel message accords with the loftier strivings and aspirations of the human race and declares that the artisans of peace are blessed "for they shall be called children of God" (Mt 5:9). The Council calls on Christians to cooperate with all men and women in securing among themselves a peace based on justice and love and in setting up agencies for peace (cf. *Gaudium et Spes*, 77).

Peace is not merely the absence of war. Nor can it be reduced solely to the maintenance of a balance of power between enemies. It is an enterprise of justice (cf. Is 32:17). It results from that harmony built into human society by its divine founder, and actualized by people as they thirst after ever greater justice.

Peace is never attained once and for all. It must be built up ceaselessly. A firm determination to respect other people and their dignity, as well as the constant practice of fraternity and solidarity, are absolutely needed for the establishment and maintenance of peace.

The Council praises those who renounce the use of violence in the vindication of their rights and who resort to methods of defense which are otherwise available to weaker parties too, "provided that this can be done without injury to the rights and duties of others or of the community itself" (*Gaudium et Spes*, 78).

The Council laments that in spite of the fact that recent wars have wrought physical and moral havoc on our world, conflicts still rage on and produce their devastating effect day by day somewhere in the world. Modern weapons threaten to lead the combatants to a savagery far surpassing that of the past (n. 79). Moreover, the arms race is an utterly treacherous trap for humanity and one that injures the poor to an intolerable degree (n. 81).

War should be banned and international action should be intensified for the avoidance of war (n. 82).

PONTIFICAL COUNCIL FOR
JUSTICE AND PEACE

The Second Vatican Council directed that some agency of the universal Church be set up for the worldwide promotion of justice and peace (cf. *Gaudium et Spes*, 90). In 1967 Pope Paul VI set up the Pontifical Commission "Justice and Peace." At the reform of the central organs of the Church, the Roman Curia, in 1988, this dicastery was renamed Pontifical Council for Justice and Peace.

Its assignment is to work for the promotion of justice and peace in the world according to the Gospel and the social doctrine of the Church. This Pontifical Council is engaged in deepening and disseminating this social thinking of the Church. It gathers information on justice and peace, development or the progress of peoples, and the respect or violation of human rights. It promotes collaboration with agencies and organizations that dedicate their attention to such themes, whether in the Church or outside it. It pays great attention to questions regarding the right to religious freedom. It has produced documents on racism, on the arms race, on the environment, and more recently on the social doctrine of the Church.

The Pontifical Council therefore takes initiatives to conscientize people in favor of peace, especially on the occasion of the World Day of Peace.

On January, 1, 1968, Pope Paul VI celebrated the World Day for Peace. He proposed that the first day of January each year be specially dedicated to peace. Pope John Paul II has continued this custom, so that on January 1, 2001, the thirty-fourth World Day of Peace was celebrated.

For this event, the Pope writes a *Message* generally running to about twenty pages, dedicated to a special topic. Some of the themes treated these thirty-four years are the following: peace is possible, education for peace, truth and peace, peace as a gift from God, peace and youth, religious freedom, women, children, forgiveness, respect for human rights, dialogue among cultures.

The *Message*, beautifully prepared in many languages, is presented by Holy See diplomats to the Secretary-General of the United Nations Organization and organs of the UN, to heads of state and government, to ambassadors and to heads of regional political and cultural organizations. It is sent to every bishop in the Catholic Church for effective dissemination in the dioceses. It is also sent to other Christian leaders and to some leaders of other religions.

In Rome, the Holy Father celebrates a special solemn Mass in which the diplomatic corps accredited to the Holy See takes a prominent part. Prayers are offered for peace in the world. Many dioceses arrange detailed programs for their local celebration.

In these ways the Catholic Church strives to get the message of peace to trickle down and reach the person in the pew.

ENCOURAGEMENT OF INTERRELIGIOUS COLLABORATION FOR PEACE

The Catholic Church attaches great importance to interreligious collaboration in the promotion of peace. She exhorts Catholics through dialogue and collaboration with the followers of other religions, and in witness of Christian faith and life, to promote spiritual and moral values and to join all peacemakers in pleading for peace and working to bring it about (cf. *Nostra Aetate*, 2; *Gaudium et Spes*, 78).

The first step toward promoting such collaboration is that believers should know one another better. In fact, the Pontifical Council for Interreligious Dialogue was established in 1964 by Pope Paul VI precisely in order to promote such knowledge with a view to mutual respect and collaboration. This Pontifical Council, and the Pontifical Council for Justice and Peace already presented, have established many contacts with other Christians and other believers and also with organizations, such as UNESCO and the World Conference on Religion and Peace, in efforts to educate for peace.

The Pope strongly encourages such initiatives. In his 1992 *Message for the World Day of Peace* he made this clear: "Interreligious contacts, together with ecumenical dialogue, now seem to be obligatory paths, in order to ensure that the many painful wounds inflicted over the course of centuries will not be repeated, and indeed that any such wounds still remaining will soon be healed. Believers must work for peace, above all by the personal example of their own right interior attitude, which shows outwardly in consistent action and behaviour. Serenity, balance, self-control, and acts of understanding, forgiveness and generosity have a peace-making influence on people's surroundings and on the religious and civil community" (*Message*, 6).

ACTION BY SOME RECENT POPES

Even a passing reference to some of the action taken by recent Popes to prevent war and guarantee peace is enough to convince anyone that the popes are really positive promoters of peace.

≈ Pope St. Pius X (1903–1914) did all he could to prevent the outbreak of the First World War. He did not succeed and who knows if this did not quicken his death.

≈ Pope Benedict XV (1914–1922) appealed against that terrible war right from his first Encyclical Letter, *Ad Beatissimi*, on November 1, 1914.

≈ Pope Pius XII (1939–1958), elected at the vigil of the Second World War, engaged himself from the start to prevent the scourge, and when it unfortunately broke out, to reduce its horrors and at the same time to indicate ways to its resolution. His Christmas Radio Messages during the war years were famous. (Those were the days before television.) Already quoted is the famous passage in his August 24, 1939, Radio message: "Nothing is lost by peace. Everything can be lost by war."

❧ Blessed Pope John XXIII (1958–1963) in 1962 intervened during the Cuba Missile Crisis between the United States and the Soviet Union to avoid what could have been a nuclear war. The following year he issued his Encyclical Letter, *Pacem in Terris*, on establishing universal peace in truth, justice, charity, and liberty.

❧ Pope Paul VI (1963–1978) is famous for his "Never War Again" address to the United Nations Plenary Assembly on October 4, 1965, during the last session of the Second Vatican Council. As the youngest Bishop at that session, I still remember how the bishops at the Council had a keen sense that history was being made when the Holy Father entered the Council hall on his return to Vatican City from New York.

❧ Pope John Paul II has spoken again and again, met government leaders, academicians, and the common people, and traveled the length and breadth of the globe as a messenger of peace. He lent the services of the Holy See to mediate and effectively prevent an imminent border conflict between Argentina and Chile. When Britain and Argentina were at war over the Falklands, he went to both countries and spoke of "the absurd and always unjust phenomenon of war." When the Gulf War was threatening, he said in his 1990 Christmas Message that "war is an adventure without return." In his address to the Diplomatic Corps accredited to the Holy See in January 1991 he stated that "peace obtained with arms would only lead to preparation for fresh violence." Pope John Paul II has often appealed for solidarity with the people of Iraq suffering under an embargo.

ACTION FOR PEACE BY
CATHOLICS WORLDWIDE

Not perhaps hitting the headlines and the front pages of newspapers, but no less important, is action for peace taken by Catholics all around the world. There are lay faithful who work in parliaments, universities, trade unions, and less-known venues to build peace. There are Catholic lay movements that sacrifice time, personnel, and resources in order to persuade warring parties to come to the conference table. There are medical doctors, nurses, and other voluntary workers who risk death in order to come to the aid of refugees, wounded soldiers, and populations near war-ravaged areas. These are all blessed because they are peacemakers and shall be called children of God (cf. Mt 5:9).

There are Bishops like Bishop Gerardo Flores Reyes of Vera Paz, Guatemala, who together with the Apostolic Nuncio, helped persuade the government to meet the guerrillas and the minority Indians and make peace. This Church mediation is believed to have helped toward the international recognition of the Indian cause and indirectly in the awarding of the Nobel Prize for Peace to Rigoberta Menchu. In the Republic of Benin in West Africa the extraordinary action of Archbishop Isidore de Souza helped avert internal strife and pave the way to a democratic resolution of opposing stands. The action of the Catholic Church, especially as led by Cardinal Sin of Manila, helped toward a peaceful transfer of presidential power in the Philippines in 1986 and 2001.

As already hinted, we must not underrate the witness value for peace which the lives of monks and nuns, religious brothers and sisters of the Catholic Church, do make. These consecrated people, without words, teach people the values of simplicity of lifestyle, detachment from earthly goods, hard and honest work, willingness to share, and love of others as brothers and sisters.

ST. FRANCIS OF ASSISI, MAN OF PEACE

St. Francis of Assisi is a model Christian who shows us how to witness to and promote peace. St. Francis loved peace. He lived it. He preached it. He was against war, even if the aim of the war was to recover the places where Jesus lived and died. In this, Francis went against the prevailing current in his time, both in relations between Assisi and surrounding towns, and in Christian-Muslim relations in the wider world.

St. Francis was no superficial pacifist. He was not pursuing a slogan. He was living the Christian teaching of God the Creator and Father of all men and women, and Jesus the Savior of all and the brother of all.

Peace, as said earlier in this book, is dear to religions. *Shalom, pax tecum, śāntih,* and *Al-salámu 'alaykum* are the usual greetings among Jews, Christians, Hindus, and Muslims. It is no wonder that in the yearning of humanity to promote a culture of peace in this third millennium, St. Francis of Assisi has a special appeal to people of many religions. He teaches them how to join hands to prepare for a more peaceful world. Such a message, seriously believed in and authentically lived, cannot but attract the attention of Christian mystics, Buddhist ascetics, Muslim sufis, and Hindu gurus. It is no surprise that this medieval saint is of such great relevance today in encouraging interreligious initiatives for peace.

Freedom of Religion
Needed for Peace

These reflections cannot be brought to an end without a consideration of the importance that respect for the right to religious freedom in the building of peace. This respect is so crucial that where it is missing, or where it is ignored or, worse still, deliberately violated, it becomes very difficult for the people of the various religions to contribute to peace in the ways so far envisaged.

MEANING OF RELIGIOUS FREEDOM

To practice religion in a way worthy of the human person, freedom is necessary. A human being needs to be free from constraint coming from individuals or associations, or even from legitimately constituted authority, whether local or national, religious or civil. Religious freedom is a right, a moral claim made on other people, and a necessary climate for collaboration with other believers to build a harmonious society.

"This freedom," says the Second Vatican Council, "means that all men are to be immune from coercion on the part of individuals and of social groups and of any human power, in such wise that in matters religious no one is to be forced to act in a manner contrary to his own beliefs, whether privately or publicly, whether alone or in association with others, within due limits" (*Dignitatis Humanae*, 2).

Religious freedom includes not only freedom of conscience, but also freedom to live, profess, and spread one's religion, alone or with others.

BASIS FOR RELIGIOUS FREEDOM

The human person is created in the image and likeness of God, is endowed with reason and free will, and is therefore privileged to bear personal responsibility. The human person is by nature impelled and morally bound to seek the truth, especially religious truth, to adhere to the truth when it is known, and to order personal life in accord with the demands of that objective truth. This confers on the human person a high dignity and a demanding responsibility.

To be able to live up to these demands, the human person needs immunity from external coercion. The right to religious freedom is founded on the dignity of the human person, as we can learn both from reason and from divine revelation (cf. Vatican II, *Dignitatis Humanae*, 2; John Paul II, *Address to Diplomats* 7, on Jan. 9, 1989, in *L'Osservatore Romano* Weekly Eng. Ed., Feb. 13, 1989, p. 3).

It follows that since the human person is social by nature, inner acts of religion require external expression. Such external expression should also enjoy the same immunity from coercion as the inner acts. In itself the external expression could be individual. But since man is a social being, he seeks to live out his life in association with others. So in religious matters, his freedom should be exercised in common worship, with the possibility of forming religious associations and of allowing his religious convictions to shape his life in society. Religion is not just a private affair. Therefore religious freedom cannot be restricted to the purely personal domain.

RELIGIOUS PLURALITY, TOLERANCE, ACCEPTANCE, COLLABORATION

Since religious plurality is a fact in this world of ours, it becomes necessary that people should learn to tolerate others who have different religious convictions, to accept them, to respect them, and to be ready to work with them in order to build peace.

The term *religious tolerance* can sound negative when it seems to suggest that another religion is a kind of evil to be tolerated, or to be allowed to exist with regret and only within laid-out limitations. Yet religious tolerance can be given a positive and much more acceptable connotation. It would then mean respect for other religious persuasions, acceptance of their followers, and readiness to work with them. Acceptance need not mean approval of all they hold or do. It just refuses to impose uniformity in matters religious. In other words, we are speaking of the freedom every human person should enjoy in religious matters, in affairs of conscience.

Even in a nuclear family, the effort to reduce everyone to the anonymity of matches in a box will not succeed in bringing peace and harmony. Each member has to be accepted and respected for what he or she is. The problem becomes more acute in a religiously pluralist society. The believer who is not able or willing to work with people of a different religious persuasion is fundamentally immature. We all know the story of the rabbi who taught his disciples that the way to know whether you are now in the daylight and no longer in the dark, is not when you can distinguish a dog from a sheep, or a fig from a vine, but rather when you can look on the face of other human beings and have enough light in you to recognize them as brothers and sisters.

RESPECT FOR RELIGIOUS FREEDOM IS NECESSARY FOR PEACE

Where there is freedom of religion, there is the foundation for contentment, fairness, justice, peace, removal of tension, encouragement to cooperation, harmony, and unity in diversity. When the followers of one religion are discriminated against, or worse still persecuted, there develops a situation of intolerance, tension, rivalry, violence, and possibly war. Moreover, when religions do not live in mutual acceptance and harmony, there is good ground for religious indifferentists and atheists to mock religion in general and to blame religions for many of the ills of society.

If we want peace, we must therefore respect other people in matters religious. As an essential requirement of the dignity of every human person, religious freedom is a cornerstone of the structure of human rights. As Pope John Paul II puts it: "The civil and social right to religious freedom, inasmuch as it touches the most intimate sphere of the spirit, is a point of reference of the other fundamental rights and in some way becomes a measure of them" (*Message for World Day of Peace*, 1988, n. 1).

Religious freedom is therefore an irreplaceable factor in the good of individuals and of the whole of society in the construction of peace. Indeed Pope John Paul II declared that "every violation of religious freedom, whether open or hidden, does fundamental damage to the cause of peace" (*Message*, 1988, introd.).

Does everyone in the world accept this principle of religious freedom and practice it? Not quite. The world would be a much happier and more peaceful place if all did respect this right. Let us see how some have tried to avoid respecting it, exaggerating to the right, or to the left, or by becoming extremist or violent.

DREAM OF ONE SOCIETY, ONE RELIGION

There are those who think that the best way to promote social cohesion is to have only one religion in any given society. If by society here one means a family or a monastery, no one would quarrel with this idea. But what the protagonists mean is a nation, a country, or a modern independent state or a particular segment of it. If, by some miracle, everyone within a modern state freely professed only one religion, while each person retained full freedom to change religion at any time, then there would be no problem of social cohesion as far as concerns religion. But where does such a miracle take place today? And what would be the lot of immigrants and visitors?

The fact is that advocates of "one state, one religion" soon find themselves perplexed, because although there may be a majority religion in a particular society or country, there are also other religions professed by some people in the same territory. The temptation to religious intolerance is an easy one. Efforts to impose one religion on everyone may then be made directly by proselytism that relies on force and pressure, or indirectly by the denial of certain civil or political rights. It may lead to a policy of exclusion of those who do not conform. The identification of religious law with civil law can easily stifle religious freedom. Some of the symptoms are vilification of other religions through the mass media or in religious teaching or preaching, stereotyping, reduction of other believers to the status of second-class citizens, and general tension. In one country the extremists even made out a list of words which other religions were not allowed to use!

The thesis of one state, one religion is flawed because it violates the great principle of freedom of conscience and of religion which is a major fundamental right of the human person. It irreverently ignores the fact that religion should well up from the human soul as a free response to God the Creator and as a free offering. De facto efforts to impose one religion on people have not produced the desired peace and harmony but rather tension, resistance, and readiness for martyrdom.

Attend Only to Factors Common to Religions

A totally different approach to the challenge of religiously pluralist societies is the view of those who think that the best way to promote social harmony in such societies is to pay attention only to what all religions have in common. They think that it is possible to sift out a few common elements from all the religions existing in a society and to build on these elements. They talk of a common code of conduct, consensus morality, and agreed ethical standards. They indeed do not ask that religions be abolished, but they consider it fanatical and divisive to speak of particular religions. For them, beliefs are not important. The politically correct stance is to be liberal toward all and not to be weighed down by particular religious convictions or beliefs.

In reply I would like to say that it is true that natural philosophy or right reason, without any particular religious affiliation, can arrive at certain truths of the moral or ethical order which all human beings can share. One thinks of ethics as developed by Plato or Aristotle. But in practice today it will be found that in actual life the ethical codes that guide people are set in religious contexts. A general or vague statement of agreed ethical norms will not be able to sustain people at critical moments of life or when they are faced by some major temptation. For such crises, a religion that gives a worldview and a complete philosophy of life is necessary. This is another way of saying that ethical norms are built on belief systems and are nourished and invigorated by a religion that also sustains itself by ritual celebrations. The proposal of ethical norms based on the religion of nobody cannot carry anybody across the long and exacting pilgrimage of life. Indeed it smacks of secularism, which ignores or marginalizes all religions, or at least regards religion as a personal and private matter that should not be discussed in public.

There must be available a way to social cohesion that

respects the human being and the right to freedom of religion, that takes religions seriously and that nevertheless offers a dynamic formula to promote harmony in society.

RELIGIOUS EXTREMISM, FANATICISM, OR FUNDAMENTALISM

In facing, or rather refusing to face, the fact of religious plurality, some people adopt a more radical stand. They are the religious extremists, fanatics, or fundamentalists.

Such people declare that only their religion should exist in their country or state, to the exclusion of other religions. They go further and give their religion an interpretation or cast which they consider to be its original or pure form. That is the only form they regard as legitimate. Sometimes they do not hesitate to use violence and to kill or marginalize people, including more moderate members of their own religious community, all in their effort to promote their own idea of their religion. They are therefore rightly called religious fanatics, or extremists, or, less correctly, fundamentalists. I say "less correctly" because they are really not good and authentic interpreters of their religious tradition.

Religious extremism is wrong. It is not right to try to supress all freedom to religious diversity. In any case, it is a venture doomed to failure. Religion should be proposed, not imposed. Religion should well up from the human heart as a free response to God's call recognized by conscience in search of truth about the Creator.

The Catholic Church, in the document *Dignitatis Humanae* already quoted, insists on the right of the human person to religious freedom. Much as Catholics may wish to share their faith with others, Canon Law says expressly: "It is never lawful for anyone to force others to embrace the Catholic faith against their conscience" (Canon 748, ø 2).

The Qur'an emphasizes that there is no compulsion to believe and that forced faith is not real faith: "There is no compulsion in religion" (Q 2, 256). "Will thou then compel mankind against their will to believe?" (Q 10, 99).

The Secretary-General of the U. N., Mr. Kofi Annan, speaking as already reported to one thousand religious representatives in the U. N. assembly hall on August 29, 2000, emphasized the importance of respect for people's fundamental right to freedom of religion, to worship, to build places of worship, to write, publish, and teach, etc. He added: "The Member States of the United Nations have enshrined these freedoms in several landmark documents, most notably the Universal Declaration of Human Rights. Where governments and authorities fail to protect these freedoms, it is at once an affront and a menace. Where religions and their adherents are persecuted, defamed, assaulted, or denied due process, we are all diminished, our societies undermined. There must be no room in the twenty-first century for religious bigotry and intolerance."

It is not difficult to see that religious fanaticism causes tension, unnecessary suffering, and violence. Whether the religious fanatic is in good faith or bad faith, harm is done to justice and peace. Far-seeing religious leaders and wise statesmen are needed to convince people that freedom of religion is one of the dearest of human rights and is indispensable for peace. Education for peace should take due note of this basic form of observance of the Golden Rule and of practicing genuine religion.

RECIPROCITY

The right to religious freedom is, as earlier observed, based on the dignity of the human person as created by God. The exercise of this right should therefore have no territorial boundaries. It applies wherever there is a human being. People of the majority religion in a country should not therefore deny to religious minorities in that country the very freedom of religion that they claim for their coreligionists in another country where they are in the minority. This is what reciprocity is all about.

In order to build for peace, we need the acceptance and practice of reciprocity. Understood in the negative sense, reciprocity can mean vindictiveness or vendetta, a type of religious tit for tat. It is reflected in the attitude: If you give my religion freedom in your country, I will give your religion freedom in my country. If you speak or write against us, we will pay you back in the same coin. If you kill some of our coreligionists, we will kill some of yours. This attitude is unacceptable. It is unworthy of anyone who believes in God. Let us remember that God lets his rain fall on the fields of both the just and the unjust. For a Christian in particular, the teaching of Jesus Christ is clear: "Offer the wicked man no resistance. On the contrary, if anyone hits you on the right cheek, offer him the other as well" (Mt 5:39). This is a way of teaching that we should not repay evil with evil.

Reciprocity, taken positively, is equivalent to calling for observance of the Golden Rule: Treat others as you want them to treat you. If you want your religion to have places of worship in another country where another religion is that of the majority, you must concede the same right to religious minorities in your own country. The same thing is to be said regarding preaching one's religion and receiving converts from another religion. The one necessary condition is that all proselytism be avoided, that is, that the means adopted to win converts be noble, true, honest, and respectful of human dignity and freedom.

On June 21, 1995, the day on which the first mosque was being inaugurated in Rome, Pope John Paul II spoke of the necessity of reciprocity in the general audience. "A grand mosque is being inaugurated in Rome today. This event is an eloquent sign of the religious freedom recognized here for every believer. And it is significant that in Rome, the center of Christianity and the See of Peter's Successor, Muslims should have their own place of worship with full respect for their freedom of conscience. On a significant occasion like this, it is unfortunately necessary to point out that in some Islamic countries similar signs of the recognition of religious freedom are lacking. And yet the world, on the threshold of the third millennium, is waiting for these signs! Religious freedom has now become part of many international documents and is one of the pillars of contemporary society" (in *L'Osservatore Romano*, Weekly Eng. Ed., June 28, 1995, p. 11).

RESPECT FOR RELIGIOUS IDENTITY

Respect for the religious identity of other believers should go hand in hand with initiatives to work together with them to promote peace. This plea for interreligious collaboration for peace should not be misunderstood or misinterpreted to mean support for the foundation of more religions. A supermarket of religions is not being suggested. We already have far too many religions. To make the stage even more complicated, there are sects and pseudo-religious or esoteric groups which are striving for recognition on a par with long-established religions. Nevertheless, much as it might be beautiful if there were only one religion, we should not deny any human being the exercise of the right to religious freedom, within due limits (cf. Vatican II, *Dignitatis Humanae*, 2).

To argue in favor of interreligious collaboration, on the other hand, does not aim at depriving any religion of its identity. It is not an effort to persuade the various religions to cast their beliefs, rites, and moral codes into a melting pot for the brewing of a syncretistic product, a lowest-common-denominator religion. Such a religion would be the religion of nobody. Meant to fit anybody, it could not offer anyone a dynamic and satisfactory philosophy of life, a clear enough road map. It would not stand anyone in good stead in a moment of great moral crisis.

Interreligious cooperation presumes that the participating believers belong each to a religion with clear self-identity. Such a genuine religion should be one that has clear beliefs, ritual, and code of conduct. It should equip the believer with a unified view of life. It should present a vital synthesis of the details that make up a person's daily life. The Second Vatican Council, for example, tells Catholics that there must be no false opposition, but rather a unity, between their professional and social activities on the one hand, and their religious life on the other. "In the exercise of their earthly activities," it insists, "they can thereby gather their humane, domestic, professional, social and technical enterprises into one vital synthesis with religious values, under whose supreme direction all things are harmonized unto God's glory" (*Gaudium et Spes,* 43). In short, religion is not a special coat put on for one hour on Sunday morning. It is a life which we live twenty-four hours a day, seven days a week.

Only a person so calmly and deeply rooted in a religion can properly work with other believers to promote peace.

RIGHT TO SPREAD ONE'S RELIGION, BUT WITH FAIR MEANS

As said earlier, the right to religious freedom includes the right to share one's religion with other people. Both individuals and religious bodies have this right to seek to share their way of life with others who freely welcome it. For Christians, this is called evangelization, sharing the Good News of Jesus Christ with other people, preaching Jesus Christ, and offering others an opportunity to receive the Gospel. For those who freely listen, this is their right. For the Christian it is not only a right but a duty to share the faith.

It is therefore unacceptable that some people should oppose the right of Christians, or indeed of any other believers, to propose their religion to others in all freedom. Such a stand should be regarded as religious fanaticism or fundamentalism and should be rejected. It is opposed to the right of the human person to religious freedom, as also recognized by the United Nations Organization in paragraph 18 of its 1948 Universal Declaration of Human Rights.

At the same time we should repeat what has been said earlier in this book: that in proposing one's religion to other people, the methods used should be in accordance with justice and truth; they should respect the freedom and dignity of other people and the rights of other religious bodies. As the Second Vatican Council says: "In spreading religious faith and in introducing religious practices, everyone ought at all times to refrain from any manner of action which might seem to carry a hint of coercion or of a kind of persuasion that would be dishonourable or unworthy, especially when dealing with poor or uneducated people. Such a manner of action would have to be considered an abuse of one's own right and a violation of the right of others" (*Dignitatis Humanae*, 4).

Indeed, it is opposed to the nature of religion and of truth that force or tricks be used on people to bring them to change their convictions. "The truth cannot impose itself except by virtue of its own truth, as it makes its entrance into the mind, at once quietly and with power" (op. cit., 1).

Proselytism is the effort to persuade a person to embrace a religion by methods that offend against human dignity or that exploit the weakness or difficult situation of that person. Examples would be to try to "convert" a person to a religion by force or pressure, whether such pressure be physical, psychological, political, economic, or otherwise. To entice a person to a religion in order to give that person a study scholarship, or a job opportunity, or promotion, or simply food or money, is also proselytism. This is wrong because it does not respect the God-given dignity and freedom of the human person. Religious unity arrived at by means of force, or pressure, or clever maneuvering, is not worthy of humanity and is not a suitable gift for Almighty God. Genuine religion should be a free response of the human soul to God the Creator.

It is clear that proselytism is disrespectful of human dignity and freedom and so is not conducive to harmony and peace. On the other hand, the proposal of one's religion to others in a climate of freedom and respect is not only not opposed to peace, but is rather a dimension of that freedom, tranquillity, and possibility of choice which are needed for a dignified and enduring peace.

RESPONSIBILITY OF PUBLIC AUTHORITIES

It is not enough that all agree that the individual, or a group of people, has the right to religious freedom. Provision has to be made for the exercise of this right. The public authorities have a duty here.

Public authorities should facilitate and guarantee the right of citizens—individuals or groups—to religious freedom. They should protect them and encourage their collaboration with citizens of differing religious convictions in building up their country. Public authorities should promote justice, impartiality, and peace and thereby help to reduce or abolish tension, discrimination, intolerance, and religious persecution.

On January 12, 1993, the Council of Europe in a Report on Religious Tolerance in Democratic Societies wisely recommended that "the secular state should not impose any religious obligations on its citizens. It should also encourage respect for all recognized religious communities and promote them in their relations with society as a whole" (cf. UNESCO, *Istanbul Symposium Working Document*, 1995, p. 128). Given that in some countries the exercise of the right to religious freedom is made difficult or well-nigh impossible for some people, pressure could be put on the governments of these countries to improve their record and facilitate harmony.

No doubt governments are competent over matters touching the common good such as fair state laws, taxes, justice and peace among citizens, and social harmony in general. But in purely religious matters, public authorities have no competence. Religious leaders should not allow religion to be used or manipulated by politicians. Religion should be allowed necessary freedom to concentrate on beliefs, ritual, and a rule of life. God is at the center of all genuine religion. Politicians and governments should be impartial toward all religions. Religious leaders who succumb to the temptation of allowing their religion to be abused and made an instrument by a political party will have to reflect on the negative consequences, including the probability that that religion is likely to become a despised widow when that political party is no longer in power. At times it will be useful for religious and political leaders to meet and discuss such questions.

Anyone who reflects on the matter will appreciate how important due respect for competences is for harmony and peace in society.

HUMANITY HAS PROGRESSED
IN THIS APPRECIATION

Humanity has come a long way through history in the appreciation of the right of the human person to religious freedom and the importance of this recognition for social harmony and peace. Even the famous document of the Second Vatican Council on this right, *Dignitatis Humanae*, quoted several times in this work, was not a sudden product. It came as a result of a slow maturation that had been taking place in the Catholic Church. This has been going on since the very beginnings when her divine Founder Jesus Christ, meek and humble of heart (cf. Mt 11:29), offered his Good News of Salvation to people but did not use force (cf. Mk 16:16; Mt 11:28–30; Jn 6:67–68), to the years when the Catholic faith became dominant and a heretic was considered by the Inquisition to be a dangerous citizen, through the period of the French Revolution and the challenge of illuminism and rationalism, to the more balanced stance of modern democratic societies. *Dignitatis Humanae* is hailed as one result of a healthy development of doctrine. St. Vincent of Lerins likened such development to human growth where "the tiny members of unweaned children and the grown members of young men are still the same members." So, says the saint, "there should be vigorous progress in the understanding of truth of revelation with the passing of the ages and the centuries, but only along its own line of development, that is, with the same doctrine, the same meaning and the same import" (St. Vincent of Lerins, *The Development of Doctrine*, Cap. 23, in PL 50, 667–668).

It would be a blessing for society if every religion also made progress in the appreciation of the importance of leaving everyone and every community free in religious matters. This would be a great contribution by the religions of the world toward the building of a more harmonious and peaceful society.

Peace Promotion:
A Task for All

As we come toward the conclusion of these reflections, we are reinforced in our conviction that the religions of the world have an irreplaceable role to play in the building of that desirable cathedral called peace, and also in the maintenance of that structure.

There is, however, neither the desire not the wish to exaggerate. I am not suggesting that cooperation among religions is enough for the promotion of peace. The enterprise of peace building is far too complicated and demanding to be carried out by religions alone.

For a just and lasting peace we also need all-around development, especially in such sectors of life as agriculture, health, and education. A certain minimum of economic